WALKING FOR FITNESS AND PLEASURE

by

Dr. Ronald E. Walker

A Hearthstone Book

Carlton Press, Inc.　　　　　　　New York, N.Y.

©1988 by Dr. Ronald E. Walker
ALL RIGHTS RESERVED
Manufactured in the United States of America
ISBN 0-8062-3230-7

INTRODUCTION
TAKE TIME TO SMELL THE ROSES!

Imagine sitting on the edge of your beach towel at the beach. Tilt your head up and face the bright sunshine. Feel the warmth cover you. Now gaze at the smooth waves crashing to shore.

In the distance you can hear children laughing, people talking, some music on a radio. You close your eyes and hug your knees closer to your body. The work week fades away with each deep, relaxing breath you take.

Suddenly, you become aware of a pleasant sensation. Your toes are wiggling in the sand. The dry granules tickle as they slide between your toes. You dig your feet into sand, down past the warmer, dry sand and into the cool, denser sand.

You begin to think that you can't remember the last time you were barefoot in the sand. You enjoy the flood of warm, happy memories. And then, filled with those warm feelings, you get up and walk toward the sea.

You stand and let the white water swirl over your feet, teasing yourself with the cool of the water. You look down at the shiny wet toes. The receding water seems to pull at your heels, moving you toward the sea. You breathe in the healthy salt smell.

Then you turn and begin walking alongside the water, letting its tide roll over your feet sometimes, other times dancing away. You walk and walk, filled with enjoyment. You only become aware of the smile on your face when you notice other walkers who pass you smiling back.

Your arms sway rhythmically at your sides. You feel your hips loosen and your stride lengthen. You imagine that you could walk on like this forever.

Lord, who would live turmoiled in the court,
And may enjoy such quiet walks as these?
—William Shakespeare

CONTENTS

One: Man's Best Medicine 9
Two: Walking—How It Works 26
Three: The Physiology of Walking 41
Four: These Shoes Were Made For Walking 51
Five: Walking Health 57
Six: Nutrition 67
Seven: Advanced Walking 79
Eight: Get Out and Walk! 83
Special Reference Section: Walker's Injuries 88
References 112

WALKING FOR FITNESS AND PLEASURE

Chapter One

Man's Best Medicine

Walking, walking. To stride and stride again. Your short walk at the beach was only the beginning. The greatest revelation to take from that day is that you don't need the warm sun shining down on the sand to fully enjoy walking. Walking IS forever.

Whether you walk along the shore, or through deep forests with overhanging trees, or through the local shopping mall with its bright lights and colors isn't what matters. What matters is that you are walking and by doing so you have opened a treasure trove of wonderful things for you and your body.

Did you ever think you could enjoy something that was good for you? Well, it is!! Unlike running, which multiplies the pounding stress your feet, ankles, knees, hips and back have to endure, walking is gentle and uplifting.

Imagine, when you run, your feet absorb up to three times your body weight with each jarring stride. That is like jumping off a short stool onto one foot with each stride.

Walking is civilized. Who was it that said only pain guarantees gain? Your body is a marvel of good mechanics. And no part of your body proves that any better than your feet. Yes, those lovely objects down there with the ten toes wiggling. Did you know that each foot is controlled by twenty-six bones, one hundred and seven ligaments, sixty-six joints and nineteen muscles?

No, how could you? But now that you know, aren't you amazed with those numbers? And the best part is—all that complexity was designed so that you will be able to move about without EVER having to suffer undue pain.

Walking lets you get the 'gain' without the pain. Walking frees you from the muscle cramps and sprains, torn ligaments, bone dislocations and stress fractures jogging invites. It frees you from damaging compression of the nerves in the neck, arms, legs, and low back. It frees you from decreased sex drive, impotence and infertility brought about by poor blood supply to the testicles and ovaries.

Walking is wonderful!

Can you see yourself walking along the seashore? Smooth, fluid gait, fine breeze brushing against your arms, contented smile on your lips. You walk quickly enough to increase your pulse rate and you feel healthiness surge through your body.

It makes you wonder why anyone would ever take up jogging to begin with.

Why do they? Well, to hear a jogger tell it, jogging gives the runner untold benefits. And that, to an extent, is certainly true. But just as a bicycle can be ridden on flattened tires, it is much easier and more pleasurable to ride on inflated tires. That is, there is a better way.

The Aerobic Benefits of Walking

The runner will tell you about the aerobic benefits of running. First off, what exactly is meant by 'aerobic benefits'?

An aerobic exercise increases your heart rate and oxygen consumption, thereby making your body work better. So aerobic benefits are those that benefit your body by making your heart and lungs function more efficiently.

Sure, running is an aerobic activity. You know that, everyone knows that. But walking is too.

Remember that walk on the beach? Remember how you felt once you got into the rhythm of your stride, with your arms swinging at your sides? It felt as if good health was surging through your body. THAT was because of the aerobic benefit walking brought you.

Your heart was beating quicker and your breaths were deeper, your blood was pulsing through all the muscles you were actively using, muscles that might have been neglected for too long.

And there was an added benefit that you couldn't even feel. Actually, there were many added benefits. One of the things that aerobic activity does very effectively is burn calories. So while you were walking and feeling so good, you were actually burning up calories stored in your body's fat cells!

Getting the picture?

Let's return for a minute to that day at the beach. You probably wanted to simply get away—from the house, work, stress—whatever—away from the craziness that seems to intrude in everyone's life. And your walk along the shore was part of that. A nice 'feeling good' activity. But you're having a little bit of trouble believing that what felt so good could also be good for you.

Relax. You're not alone.

For all the wonderful things that can be said about being an American one of the negative things that is also true is that we tend to overdo things. This is true of television viewing, fashions and even seemingly 'healthy' pursuits such as dieting and exercise.

You probably tried some diet/exercise program before. And, if you are like most of us, it fell far short of your expectations and goals.

One of the reasons this is probably true is because of the myth we talked about before, you know—'no pain, no gain.' For some reason, we Americans seem to demand that our diets be sacrifices and our exercise programs be torture programs.

And, as we've already said, the result is usually more damage than good. Yet, the basic notion persists. We all hang onto it. You hang onto it. You say to yourself, "That walk was very enjoyable." And you think, "How could it have have been healthy?"

Why can't we just accept that some things can be pleasurable AND healthy? And that walking tops the list?

I have a friend, I'll call her Betty, who thought she was terribly overweight. Now, truth be known, she was only about five pounds above where she wanted to be and she looked fine. But Betty was unhappy with her weight and her appearance so she joined a local health club and had one of their 'experts' design a diet and exercise program for her.

He reduced her calories and put her in aerobic dance classes as well as working on the weight machine three times a week.

For the first month, Betty was aglow. She lost a couple of pounds quickly and her muscles toned up. She decided that if the program she was on could help her this much, working out five days a week could help her even more.

To talk with her after three months in the program, you would have thought you were talking to a religious convert. She kept trying to get all her friends to join the health club. She spoke the religion of 'sweat, pain and gain.'

About a month later, Betty twisted her ankle during aerobic dance. Nothing serious, just a bit annoying. Betty taped her ankle and kept up with her exercise routine. Within a week, she couldn't even step on her foot without pain.

She had to stop working out. She returned to her old lifestyle, gained back her weight—in fact, the only thing she gained from the experience in the long term was a deep cynicism toward exercise in general.

But through it all, even to this day, Betty maintains the 'no pain, no gain' attitude.

But you know that 'fad' diets and strenuous exercise can't be maintained for years and years. You need an activity that can fit into a long-term lifestyle. An activity that will benefit you every day.

And the only type of activity that can be long lasting must be one that is pleasurable. Like walking.

Hippocrates, the first doctor, said: "Walking is man's best medicine." He sure knew what he was talking about.

"Okay," you're saying. "You've got my attention. Tell me exactly how walking helps me."

I thought you'd never ask.

Walking and Weight Control

I talked about walking as an aerobic exercise that burns calories. What I didn't tell you is that a regular walking program also helps you control your weight by acting as a natural appetite suppressant.

Let me tell you about another friend, Marvin. Marvin is lawyer. He's in his middle thirties, is fairly successful and is very concerned about his appearance. "It makes a difference in court," he tells us.

He is constantly dieting and working out at the local gym. The problem is—whenever he is working out, his appetite seems to increase. And he rationalizes bigger meals and occasional desserts by saying that he's burning those extra calories in his gym work.

The problem is—he has increased his caloric intake so much that he is actually GAINING weight. Sure, he looks better for a while because he's toning his muscles but as soon as he stops (which he always does) that extra muscle becomes extra fat.

His exercise program actually increases his appetite.

I hate to harp on this, but Marvin's problem is actually just another ugly face of the 'no pain, no gain' monster. He works out so hard that he needs the extra calories.

When I finally convinced Marvin to try walking, he was amazed at how little he needed to eat to feel full. His weight went down and his waistline diminished.

Unfortunately, Marvin began lifting weights again and hooked himself into the pain/gain, high caloric intake routine.

But you can escape that cycle! You've already begun!

Walking Helps Slow Down the Aging Process

But what about if you're getting older? Well, I hate to sound like I've got a cure-all, but...Once again, walking fits the bill.

We all know people who, as they have aged, have become more and more sedentary. They 'accepted' old age, which meant accepting reduced energy, reduced capacity, reduced joy. But it doesn't have to be that way. Researchers have found that proper physical activity that is a part of a way of life can significantly delay the aging process.

Of course, we all get older and our bodies do change. We do experience some fatigue, decreased stamina and vigor, increased weight, some reduction in joint flexibility, changes in bowel and bladder habits, decreasing hearing and sight.

These changes vary greatly from person to person. For the most part we associate these 'aging processes' with changes that occur sometime in a person's sixties. But many of these changes have more to do with lifestyle than with age.

Researchers in Sweden took five healthy young men and put them in bed for twenty days. After that relatively short period of inactivity the researchers found that cardiac output of the men decreased dramatically, as did their oxygen uptake and their breathing capacity.

These changes were less the result of aging than of a sedentary lifestyle.

One of the most tragic consequences of living to a ripe old age is the specter of osteoporosis, loss of bone density and subsequent weakening of the bone itself. Once this occurs, then breakage of the bone is a very real threat.

Researchers have found that one way to slow down this breakdown of bone density is to exercise. Through exercise, the circulation to the bones improves and therefore the bone growing cells are stimulated. Bones stay stronger and are less likely to break.

Walking is a particularly apt exercise for this purpose because research indicates that walking strengthens the bones, especially the bones of the legs. In addition, walking promotes a greater range of motion for the arms and legs.

It is not unusual for researchers to discover that the 'bone age' of a patient is ten to twelve years younger than the chronological age of the patient.

Exercise cannot 'turn back' the clock. Nothing can. What has been shown however, is that exercise—and remember, by exercise I DO NOT mean strenuous exercise—lengthens the plateau of middle age. So, whereas you cannot expect to be eighteen again, you could conceivably 'be' fifty to sixty well into your seventies and eighties.

Cardiovascular Benefits of Walking

We all know someone who has suffered a heart attack.

I have a friend whom I'll call Frank, who used to live in the housing complex with us. He was a friendly man, always kind and helpful. It came as a surprise to me to learn that he had suffered two 'mild' heart attacks in his life. But after each, he had recovered sufficiently to return to his job as a salesperson in a fish market.

Then, one night, I heard the sirens coming closer. Frank had suffered a severe heart attack. He was unconscious when he was wheeled from his apartment but still alive.

He spent the next two weeks in an intensive care unit. The doctors refused to say anything hopeful even after the first week when he came out of the coma he'd remained in since the attack. All they would offer was "it's touch and go."

But Frank made it through those first couple of weeks and after almost a month in the hospital, he was sent home. During his convalescence, Frank was referred to a cardiologist to determine whether he would benefit from coronary bypass surgery. The doctor's report was not promising.

He declined to recommend surgery. He felt that Frank had reached almost terminal coronary heart disease. He recommended a treatment of drugs, low-sodium diet and long periods of absolute rest.

In other words, the doctor was saying: "Go home and wait for the BIG one."

Frank started to get his papers in order, make sure his life insurance policy was up to date and make sure his will was clear. But he did these things like a sleepwalker, he was so depressed.

After the period of depression which is common in most heart patients passed, Frank felt that he had to take control. He kept to the strict diet, he didn't even consider returning to work and he started walking. In spite of the doctor's instructions, he knew that he had to do something physical.

Frank didn't become a marathon walker. He didn't become the kind of person that you read about on the pages of the local paper. What he did was, he took control of his life and proceeded to try to make it better.

His walks began at about half a block. Before long he was walking a mile and then two miles a day. When I accompanied him on one of these walks, I was amazed at how cheerful he was.

Walking may not have been totally responsible for Frank's improvement and sense of well-being, but I am convinced, and research seems to bear us out, that his careful, modest exercise program was instrumental in improving his condition.

How does walking help the cardiovascular system? Well, before answering that, it would be a good idea to describe exactly how the cardiovascular system works.

Central to the system are your heart and lungs. Your heart is a powerful muscle that pumps your blood throughout your body. Your lungs take this blood and clean it—that is, they take the carbon dioxide from your blood and replace it with oxygen. Then the blood is pumped through your veins and arteries, carried to each and every last cell in your body.

The more efficiently your body pumps blood, the more efficiently each and every cell of your body receives its 'food.' If your heart muscle is weak or if you have 'too many' cells (if you're overweight) then the system doesn't work efficiently.

Because your heart is a muscle like all other muscles in your body, it can be strengthened like any other muscle. But, whereas push-ups might be all right for chest and shoulder muscles, a different exercise is needed for the heart.

Heart exercise means increasing the number of beats your heart takes per minute (but not increasing them too much). As your heart gets stronger, it needs fewer beats per minute to do its job because the beats are more powerful. This is what is meant by aerobic activity. Your heart and lungs are exercising so they can function more efficiently.

How do you know how many beats per minute your heart should beat to get the maximum benefit and the minimum danger? Doctors have come up with something called the TARGET HEART RATE (rate meaning beats per minute). To calculate your target rate you simply subtract your age from 220 (so if you are forty years old you end up with 180). This is your maximum heart rate. To find out your heart rate you take 75% of your maximum heart rate. So, if you are forty, your target rate would be 135 beats per minute.

If you can maintain that heart rate for 15 to 20 minutes, you will be doing your heart and lungs a favor.

Walking briskly—and we will discuss "how to walk" later in the book—lets you easily and enjoyably reach your target rate and maintain it for well over the 20 minutes you would need to derive cardiovascular benefits from the walk.

An additional benefit of aerobic walking is that it can lower your blood pressure. Blood pressure is a measure of how hard your blood beats against the walls of your arteries. It helps a doctor determine how hard your heart has to work to pump blood through your body.

Walking does a couple of things to help lower your blood pressure. One, it helps you regulate your weight. Being overweight is an important factor in high blood pressure. Two, it strengthens the muscles in your lower leg, your calf muscles. These muscles have been referred to as a second heart because when they are developed and working well, they help your heart by sending the blood on its way back up through our body. Three, it helps increase the number and size of your blood vessels for better and more efficient circulation. Four, it decreases triglyceride (fats) and cholesterol levels.

Most importantly, walking decreases your DYNAMIC blood pressure, your real everyday blood pressure, not just the blood pressure reading the doctor is able to get in his office.

Your blood pressure has many peaks and valleys throughout the day, in response to all sorts of emotional and physical stimuli. Walking makes the peaks lower and the valleys higher. It relieves the stress that contributes to the changes in the dynamic blood pressure.

Stress

How often have you found yourself retreating into a quiet room just to try and 'get your thoughts sorted out'? How often does it seem like the world, with all its complexities, is encroaching on your private and comfortable life?

One of the reasons you 'escaped' to the beach that day was simply to get away from that feeling.

The problem though is in the notion that to get way from that tension is to 'escape.' It somehow implies that getting away is something that you should feel vaguely guilty about.

Remember how wonderful you felt walking along the shore? Well, that wasn't just because of your relaxing environment—it was also because of the simple fact that you were walking.

The modern world is filled with stresses of all sorts, worries about the health of family members, financial well-being, the loudness of the cars that race up and down the block late at night, even the constant yapping of the neighbor's dog.

All these annoyances, great and small, contribute to that feeling of being overwhelmed by events so that often one little thing—that proverbial straw of the camel's back—is all it takes for you to snap at the people you love and add that to the already tremendous burden of stress that you're carrying.

But you question how that walk at the beach could have really helped. You think it was just 'getting away.' But the walk did help.

Like most people, you're probably unaware of the close relationship between walking and your mind. You probably think of your mind and body as being two separate things that rarely, if ever, are directly related. You might think of them as two people who live in the same neighborhood who occasionally bump into each other on the corner, nod and then continue their different ways.

Nothing could be further from the truth.

At one time in our history, the greatest dangers we were confronted by were physical dangers—like a saber-toothed tiger jumping out at us. These dangers made our bodies adapt a system of reacting. The cerebral cortex of the brain recognized a threat and signaled the hypothalamus, which in turn switched on the nervous system stimulating the liver, which increased the blood's clotting ability—thereby reducing the likelihood of bleeding to death in the event of injury. Fat stored in the body was readied to be converted into energy. The heart rate speeded up to send extra oxygen to the muscles. Muscle tension increased to facilitate quick response. Hormones were released into the blood, allowing the body to engage in long periods of intense activity.

It was only by engaging in the physical activity for which this automatic system prepared us—that is, by fighting or fleeing—that these chemical reactions dissipated and our body systems returned to normal levels.

But, today, we are civilized. When was the last time you were confronted by a saber-toothed tiger—yet this same system of preparedness is in place. And, it goes into gear whenever we confront danger—real or imagined.

The modern world presents you with many dangers, only a small percentage of which require an immediate physical reaction. Most of the 'dangers' you are confronted with are emotional in nature. There are the demands of your job, buses and planes to catch, an argument with your husband, wife, son or daughter, social demands, anxiety about inflation, the international situation, fuel shortages and...well, just about anything and everything.

Most of these confrontations don't allow you to either fight or flee. They confront your mind. So your 'natural' reactions are either impossible or inappropriate. So you mask or bottle up your frustrations and anxieties. The natural response is thwarted and this adds to the tension.

The result is a wall of frustration, an overwhelming sense of frustration. You feel exhausted when you first get up in the morning. You kick your dog. Or worse.

This situation can lead to high blood pressure and dangerous changes in blood chemistry. These can in turn lead to a host of disorders: obesity; ulcers; colitis; muscle twitches; heart disease; cancer; a full range of disorders.

What can you do?

Take a deep breath and remember that day at the beach. Listen to the pounding of the surf. Smell the fresh salt air. Then, get up again and walk.

That's right. Walk. Walking allows you to release those hormones, it taps into that 'fight or flee' reaction and allows those pent-up stresses to drain away.

That is one of the reasons you were smiling so contentedly that day at the beach.

Depression

Sometimes the stresses and frustrations in our lives combine to create a more serious problem. Many people experience depression—which may mean anything from the blahs to severe psychosis. Depression costs our society untold millions in lost productivity, substandard products and less than satisfying services.

Over 10% of the population score in the 'depressed' range on depression questionnaires. But recent reports indicate that walking can relieve depression.

There are several reasons why this might occur. The first is that a regular walking schedule requires patience. Patience is an important factor for people who experience a sense of depression over their physical appearance, primarily if they are overweight. Patience learned through a dedicated walking routine helps the person learn and accept that physical changes take time.

Walkers learn that they can change themselves for the better. THEY are in control for the lack of a sense of control has been shown to be a significant factor in feelings of depression. One feels that because they are not in control, that they are victims. They can do nothing to change the cycle of events about which they are unhappy. Walking shows people that they have control of their lives to a sufficient degree so as to improve their health, appearance and self-image.

Walkers who maintain a dedicated regimen develop a feeling of accomplishment. This in itself is sometimes enough to correct all but the most serious forms of depression. Any time you have a sense of success and accomplishment you cannot help but feel good about yourself.

Exercise Euphoria: An Anti-Depressant

If you talk to a long distance runner, he or she is likely to relate to you the euphoria that they feel after running for 30 or 40 minutes. It is so prevalent a sensation that it is referred to as 'runner's high.'

This 'high' is a period of heightened consciousness—a period of creative, enthusiastic, excited feeling. Problems seem to recede on the far horizons of thought, cares and worries all but disappear. It's as if running had unlocked a tiny psychiatrist that lives inside the runner.

Some psychologists have suggested that this euphoric feeling is actually an altered state of consciousness, that it is an opening to the unconscious.

You can experience the same natural 'high' from a walking program. While seeing the world pass by at only three to four and a half miles per hour, you can have access to the same wonderful sensation that runners work so hard to attain.

But what is this 'high' anyway? Recent research has shown

that the brain releases a morphine-like substance into the blood in response to extended exercise. This substance is called endorphin and it is likely the source of the feelings of euphoria that walkers feel after a long invigorating walk.

Walkers have described the feeling as a wonderful release, as though they had their stresses and tensions lifted from them. In and of itself, this sense of release probably does your cardiovascular system a world of good.

But the benefits far exceed the 'high' associated with the walk. The release of tension extends long after the exercise period is over.

Sleep

Have ever experienced a sleepless night? A night of fitful sleep that makes you feel more tired in the morning than when you went to bed?

Join the ranks of millions of Americans who spend millions of hours and even more dollars in pursuit of a decent night's sleep.

Before you invest your life savings in new mattresses, relaxation tapes, sleeping pills, etc., take a moment to evaluate why you might be experiencing problems sleeping.

Some sleep problems are transient and will correct themselves. But patterns of sleeplessness are damaging. These should be dicussed with your doctor. If there is no organic cause for your sleeplessness then it is probably the result of stress and tension.

Don't allow yourself to get caught up in the cycle of medications unless it is absolutely necessary!

A friend of mine, call him Bill, was recently the victim of layoffs at the plant where he worked. He spent a couple of weeks actively seeking other employment with no luck. With each day the lines of frustration seemed to etch themselves deeper on his forehead. There were yelling matches with his wife. His son and daughter tried to make themselves scarce around the house.

And Bill found himself anxious and unable to sleep. He knew that his problems with sleep were directly related to his unemployment. But, when he put his head down on the pillow his mind would swirl with images of being poor, losing the house, never working again.

He couldn't bear the thought of himself, only forty-five years old, failing in his role as provider to his family.

He went to the doctor and told him about the situation. The doctor recommended a mild sedative to help him sleep. Bill took it but found himself feeling groggy and tired in the morning. When he mentioned he was still tired to his wife she replied that he had slept like a baby, snoring through the night. He didn't understand it. He felt tired and needed several cups of coffee to perk up.

Bill was about to begin a terrible medication cycle. But, fortunately for Bill, he had a friend who also was laid off. His friend refused to let the situation get him down and convinced Bill to join him on his morning walk.

Bill was resistant at first but then did join his friend. The first few days he had trouble keeping up but within a week he was able to sleep without medication. He felt refreshed in the morning and looked forward to the walk.

During the walk, the two friends discussed their employment situation. They focused on their years of experience and expertise. As they walked, they began to dream out loud about having their own business.

The more they walked, the clearer their vision became. After two months of job search, they decided to develop their own consulting firm.

That was three years ago. The consulting firm is still struggling but it is surviving. And the two still enjoy their morning walks when they discuss clients, the books, all aspects of their business.

Oh, and except for a rare night when Bill is preparing to meet a new client and is overly excited, he has no trouble sleeping at all.

Looking and Feeling Good

"I can't go out and exercise. Just look how my thighs and behind jiggle."

That was my friend, Janice, speaking. She wasn't very overweight. In fact, as she pointed out so succinctly, her problem has more to do with toning than anything else.

But Janice is not alone. Many people are hesitant to begin a rigorous exercise program because that will get them out of their house where they've been hiding for all the wrong reasons.

And, unless you happen to be the Duke or Duchess of Marlborough or something, chances are that your back yard isn't large enough to make walking around it enjoyable for a long length of time.

My advice to Janice? To have a little consideration for herself. She would never suggest that someone else should stay off the streets because of their appearance. Why should she condemn the most important person in her life—herself—to such a prison sentence?

Also, to have a little patience. Because walking would help her solve exactly those physical features she was less than happy about.

Watch a walker. Do you see how her arms move? How her legs stride? How erect she holds herself?

This is the icing of the cake of walking! That posture, that movement is a goal and a by-product of walking. The motion of walking firms your upper body. As much as running, it firms and strengthens your legs and buttocks—your calves, thighs, hips, buttocks, and abdomen.

Walking will strengthen ligaments and tendons, it will loosen joints, thereby easing many of those small aches and pains that seem to plague you throughout the day.

It will increase your stamina and give you more energy.

What about Janice? You probably passed her on your walk at the beach. She was the one on the towel surrounded by friends with their transistor radios playing.

If you didn't see her, she saw you and she nodded approvingly of your decision to begin to walk. She would have been the first to tell you that you were doing the right thing, the best thing.

Conclusion

Walking is like one of those mysterious boxes from the East, you know the kind—every time you open the box you find another, smaller one inside.

Walking is so accessible and simple. You simply have to get

up from your beach towel, your bench, your easy chair, whatever, and do it. And the more you do it, the more you learn about it, the better it is.

In this chapter I only wanted to convince you TO BEGIN. No book about walking matters nearly so much as your just DOING it. To this end, I have described at varying length the benefits of walking. How aerobic walking benefits:

1. the body's respiratory functions; improving lung capacity and overall cardiovascular efficiency.
2. the body's metabolism by increasing the level of oxygen in the blood stream.
3. diabetics by reducing the amount of body fat and helping the body to metabolize sugar.
4. your heart by increasing hypertension, developing muscle, getting rid of fat, improving stamina.
5. you by increasing the number of red blood cells, which can fight anemia.
6. you by seeing a preventative measure against osteoporosis.
7. you by increasing circulation to the extremities and the calf muscles, which are sometimes referred to as a 'second heart' because they assist your heart in efficient circulation.
8. your mind by offsetting depression by increasing circulation to the brain, also alleviating stress and producing better thinking ability.
9. you by assisting in muscular development and agility which results in less fatigue and more resistance to sickness.

Shall I continue? Okay, walking also benefits:
10. you by helping you maintain a more positive mental attitude.
11. you and your weight by helping you suppress your appetite.
12. your physical appearance.
13. you by helping you to sleep better and more soundly.
14. you by reducing the incidence of blood clotting

thereby reducing the risk of stroke and sudden heart attack.
15. you by improving your self image.
16. the total quality of your life.

Walking lets you appreciate your surroundings. It is an exercise that you can do alone or with friends. It is inexpensive. You do not have to schedule time on the courts or on the tee—you are your own boss.

Walking gives you time to smell the flowers. And that is what it all comes down to, isn't it?

Life is an opportunity for all of us. To live it to its fullest we must take proper care of the tools by which we must live—our bodies. We know the necessity of exercise in all this. But exercise need not be painful to be beneficial. That notion is so outmoded, it is almost prehistoric.

Indeed, it is almost the opposite that should attract us. We need exercise programs that are pleasurable enough to last us a lifetime—a long lifetime, filled with good health and many joys.

Walking is just such an exercise.

If I sound like I am on my soapbox—I AM! I am not reticent about this. I want you to walk. It will make your life better. It will strengthen your body inside and out, it will clear your mind and cleanse your soul.

If I'm not convincing enough, listen to the words of the father of modern medicine, Hippocrates: "Walking is man's best medicine." Or the words of our own great statesman, Thomas Jefferson: "Walking is the best possible exercise. Habituate yourself to walk very far."

Begin a walking program today. Get up from that beach towel, that bench, that arm chair.

Smell the flowers!

Chapter Two

Walking—How It Works

Now that I've whetted your appetite and you're ready to walk, let's explore in more detail exactly what walking is. As I said earlier, walking is a lot like those magic boxes from the Far East, the deeper you delve, the more you come up with.

On the surface of it, walking IS as simple as it looks. You've been doing it all your life. But when you think about it, of course it isn't quite that straightforward.

You can't remember when you took those first steps, advancing from the crawling stage to the toddler stage, but you've probably seen a number of small children make that transition in the years since. Remember those first tentative movements, the arms supporting and balancing the body, staggering forward and then falling—those first stages in the body's ability to balance and move. It's important to note that whereas most animals have four legs and so during their walks at least three of their feet are on the ground at any given time, the human animal has but two feet and that requires balancing each step on a single foot—a pretty impressive "feat" when you think about it.

There are some studies that show that, contrary to popular belief, even children who can walk by the age of two are really only in the beginning stages and that it isn't until the child is somewhere between seven and nine that he or she really masters the task. This is because walking requires tremendous coordination of the neuromusculoskeletal system and children who are still growing are constantly experimenting and adapting to their changing bodies and weight/height ratios.

If you have not been a walker for many years, you might actually find yourself in the curious position of having to relearn the task properly. This, of course, is not an insult. In fact, it makes perfect sense if you are planning on harnessing all the benefits walking can provide for you. Because if that is your goal, then walking deserves a place amongst other sports and exercises. And therefore, you have to understand it and have a healthy respect for it.

The first thing to understand about walking correctly is that THERE IS NO SUCH THING. That means, no two walkers walk exactly the same. Which makes sense. No two people are exactly the same.

The way you walk is as particular to you as your fingerprints. If we were to have taken a movie of your walking down the beach that day and then had a second person follow your steps—even to the point of putting their feet in your footprints—the two movies superimposed would be comical because they would be so different.

The way you walk—your walking signature—is influenced by genetic factors, height, build, the shoes you wear, mental attitude and the environment where you're walking. Can you imagine any two people sharing all these factors?

Walking is not a specific body movement or exercise as, say, a biceps curl is. Walking is a series of body movements that are cyclical in nature. That is, the movements repeat themselves over and over as long as you're walking.

Specifically, walking is a body action of moving forward while standing up straight. First one leg supports and then the other. As the body passes over each supporting leg, the other leg simultaneously swings forward in preparation for the next support phase.

Note: In order for the activity to be walking, one foot or the other is on the ground at all times. There is also a brief period when both feet are on the ground. This is referred to as the double-support phase.

While you're walking you're actually moving in three different directions (while still propelling yourself forward). With each step, your body weaves slightly side to side and rises and falls—all in a regular and harmonious way. And, while you seem to be moving forward at a constant speed, you are actually slowing down and then speeding up and again with each step.

Don't believe it? Try walking with a plate filled with water and watch the different ways the water sloshes.

Finally, while you are walking when you are supported by one foot, your pelvis shifts to the side of your other foot, and then back again. It might read as though that is a lateral motion but in fact, it is a rotational one. Your shoulders and arms also rotate in the opposite direction of the moving leg.

Now, far from a simple task, doesn't walking seem amazing? Sometimes it seems a wonder that our bodies can integrate all the separate actions and functions without falling down.

To return to a basic question: Why is walking so good for you? Because it is a dynamic action that uses almost all the body's 206 bones and 650 muscles!

Your Skeleton

To understand the dynamics of walking, let's go back to that image of the Chinese boxes. Only now, let's begin by finding the smallest one and working our way outwards. In other words, let's go to the inside of the matter and look at our skeletal structure and how it works when we walk.

As with almost any activity, the spine is the foundation. It is the trunk of your body's tree. When you walk, 26 articulated vertebrae yield and bounce back with each stride you take. Your body weight goes down your spine to your pelvic girdle. From there the femur, or thigh bone, the strongest of all your bones, carries your body weight to your shinbone and fibula. Your feet are attached to these bones and are, in effect, platforms for your whole body to balance upon.

Each of your feet contains 26 bones which distribute your weight on the base of your big and little toe and on your heel.

Healthy bones are strong and rigid because of their composition, which is half mineral (calcium, phosphorus, etc.), one quarter collagen (the same protein fiber found in your hair) and one quarter water. They are held together by strong bands of elastic tissue called ligaments.

The bones are fitted together at the joints, which are lined with cartilage and synovial fluid.

Now, if you cannot pass a basic physiology course, you can certainly understand the skeletal marvel that allows you to walk.

Muscle

The next outside box in our Chinese boxes of the body is the muscles. The muscles are laid up on the bones. They move the bones by contracting and expanding. A contracting flexor muscle pulls the bones in one direction and an extensor, or opposing, muscle draws it back.

While you walk, all the muscles of the lower body are called into play. When you start walking, the calf muscles relax and your body sways forward. Your front thigh muscles contract to bring your leg forward and to pull up the foot. When your heel strikes the ground, all your thigh and lower leg muscles contract to stabilize the knee and ankle until your body weight is pulled forward by the calf muscles. Then your hip muscles on the outside of your thigh swing your thigh forward to stabilize the leg. The trunk muscles of the abdomen, side, back and chest contract to hold your body erect so your legs can swing.

One Complete Gait Cycle of Right Limb

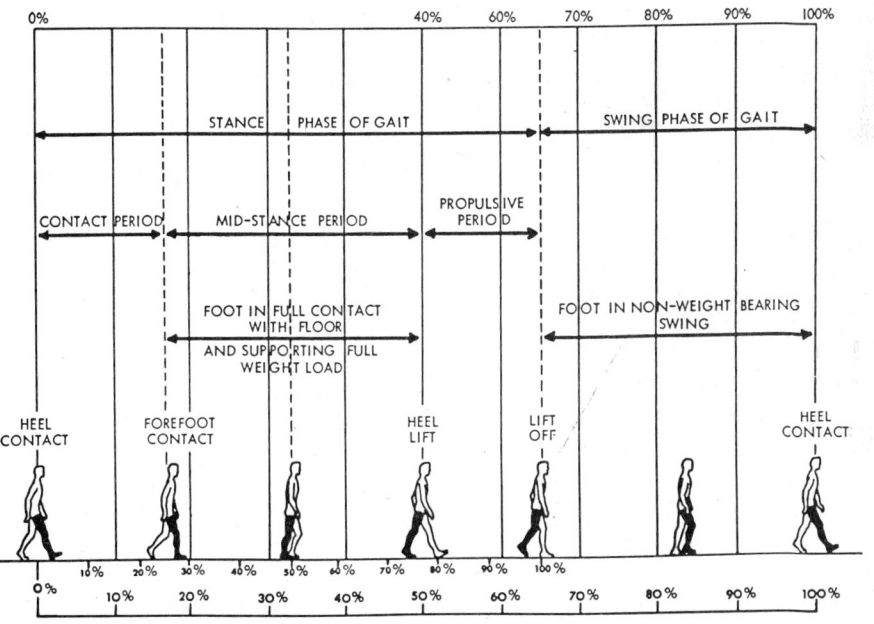

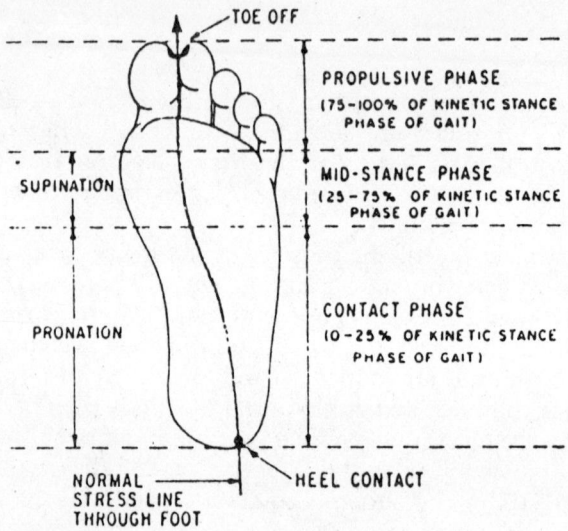

Your opposite arm swings forward by the contraction of your flexor muscles in your shoulder and forearm to counterbalance your leg swing. Then your extensor muscles contract on the return swing.

Your rear leg pushes your body forward and then swings itself forward to strike the ground heel first. Your body continues to roll forward across the ball of your foot until another push-off is begun by your rear foot. It swings forward and strikes with the heel.

This is the complete walking cycle or sequence.

It is muscular movement that circulates blood throughout your body—from the pumping of your heart which, in conjunction with the lungs sends blood to the brain and to the trunk of your body.

Remember when I talked before about walking strengthening your 'second heart?' Now you can understand more clearly what I meant. Your heart was not meant to work alone in circulating your blood through your system. It *can* do the job alone but that is overly taxing and this is an extra burden that can be damaging to the heart in the long run.

Your veins all have one-way valves spaced throughout them. These force the blood to continue moving toward the heart.

By walking and exercising your muscles, your muscular activity helps in circulating the blood by squeezing the veins and arteries and forcing the blood to move along its one-way course.

What I have called the 'second heart' is more accurately described as peripheral heart action (PHA). It is PHA that helps explain why exercise is good for the heart.

All this muscular activity benefits the muscles themselves as well. They are toned and strengthened. The fat cells in the body are burned and the increased efficiency of the circulatory system gives color and tone to your skin too.

Your Posture as You Walk

As described above, the very fact of your walking will improve your posture. But you should also be conscious of your posture while you walk.

Try to walk with your spine straight and your head held high but not so straight or so tall that you are overly conscious of it. Walking should be a natural and comfortable activity and any adjustments you make consciously should be minor.

While you are walking, don't exaggerate your arm motion. There is no need to look like a confused windmill while you walk. Walking should be a graceful, enjoyable activity.

Before you walk, take a deep breath and let your arms hang at your sides. That's right, just let them hang loosely. Now, when you start to walk, forget about them. They will swing naturally in the opposite action of your legs. If they don't, you'll fall over. Nature never intended you to fall over. They will swing.

Relax! Let your hands, hips, knees and ankles relax. And when you're walking, don't worry about the length of your stride or the movement of your hips or the motion of your head. Don't worry about anything. Enjoy it! Do whatever is comfortable. That will be what is most beneficial for your body.

And if your spine is not as straight as you think it should be, don't worry. Walking will help to strengthen the muscles in your back and that will help straighten your spine.

Your feet should strike the ground first at your heel and then up along the outer border of your foot toward your toes. You should then push off with your toes to complete the cycle.

As you walk, you will have a wonderful rolling sensation along your feet. That is good.

Try to avoid landing flat-footed or on the balls of your feet. Either of these landings could cause leg and foot problems later on.

Breathe naturally. If you breathe through your nose, continue to do so. If you breathe through your mouth, continue to do so. Just remember—the faster and longer you walk, the more air you'll need. You'll help yourself to as much as you can take in. But, and this is an important 'but,' don't get out of breath or winded. This means you're pushing too hard. Slow down. Don't forget the real beauty of walking—you get to enjoy yourself while doing great things for your body!

I have two friends, Alice and Cindi, who walk together each morning. They follow a course that leads them down the street from their houses, across a busy thoroughfare and then around the perimeter of a local golf course. The course gives them a varied scene with ponds and trees and gently rising hills. The entire course is two-and-one-half miles.

During that time, they talk about their children, recipes, the news, favorite television shows—anything and everything.

They enjoy their walks and have used them to strengthen their friendship as well as all the other benefits that come from walking.

But the reason I am reminded of Alice and Cindi now has to do with their conversations during their walks. When you walk, you should be able to carry on a conversation with a person beside you. This is a good rule of thumb to measure if you're 'over-walking.'

If you happen to enjoy walking alone—use your imagination! If someone is walking beside you, would you be able to carry on a conversation with that person while you walk? If the answer is 'no' SLOW DOWN!

Walking should be painless. If you experience any pain you should slow down, especially if the pain you feel is in your chest, neck or jaw. If slowing down doesn't relieve the pain or discomfort you feel, see your doctor. Try to take note of the circumstances when you had the pain—were you walking quickly? Were you walking up a hill? Did you spot a stray dog further down the course? Was the weather cold?

Understanding the circumstances of your discomfort can help your doctor determine the reason. Is your sock pulled tight? Your shoes laced too tightly? A muscle cramp?

If slowing down doesn't ease the pain and you can't determine any reason—see a doctor.

Finally, if you still feel excessively tired an hour or more after you've completed your walk, your walk was too strenuous. Next time out, slow down, shorten the distance, stop to smell the flowers.

Stretching

Stretching properly might be the single most important factor in any exercise program. Failure to stretch properly before *and after* exercising has probably been the cause of more people dropping out of exercise routines than any other.

Walking is no different from any other exercise in this respect. You must stretch. But don't worry—stretching isn't something that should be restricted only to those times when you exercise. Stretching can be done almost any time and almost any place—at work, in a car, waiting for a bus, under a nice shady tree, on the beach. You can stretch in the morning before the start of your day, at work to release stress and nervous tension, after sitting for a long time, whenever you feel stiff, *anytime.*

Why should you stretch? Simple. Stretching reduces tension in your muscles and makes your body feel more relaxed. It helps your coordination by allowing freer and easier movement, increases your range of motion, prevents injuries such as muscle strain, makes exercise easier because it prepares you for the activities involved. Stretching helps you develop body awareness. It promotes circulation. It makes you feel good.

Those of us who took physical education classes in school were undoubtedly taught the wrong way to stretch. Especially if you are male you probably recall 'bouncing' up and down, trying to touch your toes. This kind of stretching is dangerous at worst, pointless at best.

Muscles respond to being stretched too far (either by bouncing or overstretching). A nerve sends a signal to the muscle to contract—this is how the muscle protects itself from injury. If you stretch incorrectly, you actually tighten the muscles that you were stretching to loosen!

The proper way to stretch is GENTLY. Stretching, like walking, should get you away from the 'pain/gain' mentality.

When you stretch, you should begin your stretch by spending 10-30 seconds in a gentle stretch. DO NOT BOUNCE! Stretch to the point where you feel mild tightness and hold it at that point, trying to relax as you hold the stretch.

The tightness should begin to ease during your stretch. If it doesn't, ease off until you reach a degree of tightness that is not uncomfortable.

Remember, the goal of your stretching, like the goal of your walking program, is not to get it all done in a day. You don't have to be able to touch your toes the first day, the first week, or even the first month. What you will find by maintaining a dedicated stretching program along with your walking program is that over time your flexibility will improve dramatically. *Not immediately.* Don't push yourself.

What's the sense in hurting yourself preparing to do something that is supposed to be enjoyable?

After you have held your initial stretch through 10—30 seconds, move a fraction of an inch more until you feel the mild tightness. Again, DO NOT BOUNCE. If the tightness does not ease up—ease off slightly.

Stretching is not 'exercising' in the sense that you should not be increasing your heart rate significantly and you should not be out of breath. Your breathing should be slow, rhythmic and under control.

If you are bending forward to stretch, exhale as you bend forward and then breathe slowly as you hold the stretch. Never hold your breath while stretching.

There is no need to ever stretch a muscle beyond this additional fraction of an inch. Your goal should be long-term. You want to be limber for many years, not just for the immediate half hour after stretching.

Let stretching be enjoyable. Pick one place to stretch and try to use that place always. Try to make it a comfortable place that you like, one with no drafts. Even if the weather keeps you from walking, you can always stretch.

I will recommend just a few elementary stretches to get you started. For walking it is very important to loosen up your legs and back, shoulders and neck.

Legs

Let's begin at the bottom, at your calf. Your calf muscles are probably very tight. Most of the time we hardly notice this but you will probably be amazed at how limited your calf flexibility is.

First, face a wall or doorway that you can use for support. Take a step and a half away from this support and rest your forearms on the support with your forehead against the back of your hands. Now:

1. Bend one knee and bring it toward the support. Your back leg should be straight with the foot flat and pointed straight or even slightly pigeon toed.
2. Without changing the position of your feet, move your

hips slowly forward. Keep your back leg straight and foot flat.
3. Hold 20 seconds and then increase stretch.
4. Repeat with other leg.

This next stretch is good for your lower back, hips, groin and hamstrings. Start by standing with your feet shoulder-width apart and pointing straight ahead. Note: always keep knees slightly bent during the stretch. Locking your knees puts undue strain on your lower back. This is true of all of the stretches. Let your neck and arms relax. Now:

1. Bend forward to the point where you feel a slight tightness in the back of your legs. Hold this for about 20 seconds.

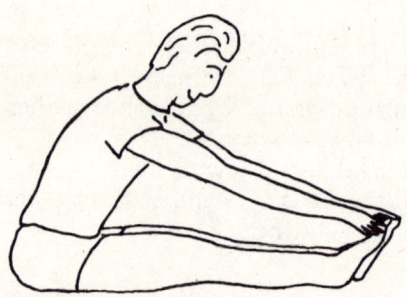

Wasn't that easy? That's the point. It's supposed to be easy. For the next stretch you will be sitting down so it's a good idea either to be in a carpeted room or to put down an exercise rug.

Sit with your legs straight and your feet upright. Your heels should be no more than six inches apart. Now:

1. Bend forward *at the hips.* Hold for 20 seconds.
2. Don't dip your head. Roll forward from the hips.
3. If you can't touch your toes, touch your knees. If you can't touch your knees, touch your thighs. Don't worry. You will get more and more limber as time goes on.

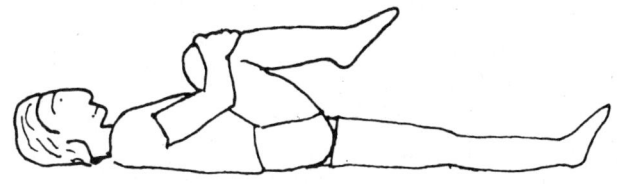

For the next stretch, lie flat on your back. Now:

1. Pull your left leg toward your chest. Keep the back of your head on the floor if possible but *don't strain*. Try to keep your right leg straight.
2. Hold for 25 seconds.
3. Now do the right leg.

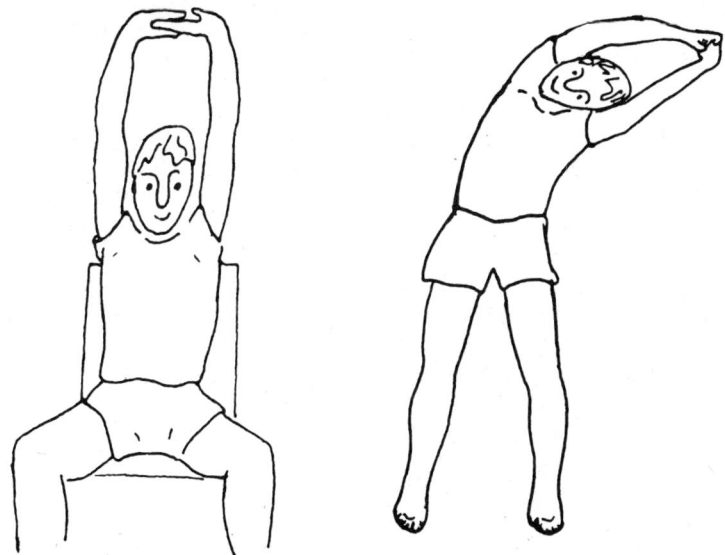

Upper Body

While sitting in a chair:

1. Interlace your fingers.
2. Turn your palms upward above your head and straighten your arms.

3. Hold for 15 seconds.
4. Repeat three or four times.

With arms overhead:
1. Hold the outside of your left hand with your right hand.
2. Pull your left arm to the side. Keep arms straight.
3. Hold for 15 seconds.
4. Repeat twice on each side.

Now, with your fingers interlaced behind your head:

1. Keep elbows straight out to the sides.
2. Keep back straight.
3. Pull your shoulder blades together gently.
4. Hold for 10 seconds.
5. Repeat several times.

For the face and neck:
1. Sit comfortably.
2. Roll your head slowly around in a circle. Keep your back straight.

These stretching exercises are only the beginning. As you increase your walking routine, your stretches should become more extensive, involving more specific muscle groups. There are many excellent books on stretching. When you are ready, avail yourself of them.

Cooling Down

Possibly the most overlooked aspect of any exercise program is the cooling down period afterwards. This is the time when you should let your body 'wind down' and readjust to its regular activity.

If you have just finished an invigorating walk, take about five minutes to walk SLOWLY, letting your heart rate slow gradually back to normal.

If you've ever lived on or visited a ranch, you know that after having horses out it is vital that they are walked before being returned to their stalls. Well, in some respects, we are like those horses. Sending yourself back to your stall without the sufficient wind-down time could put strain on your system.

Your body is constantly at work maintaining a constant body temperature. When you exercise, the way your body does this is to open the capillaries near the skin and also to perspire.

When the air hits your perspiration, it cools you down more efficiently than it could hitting dry skin. The coolness cools the blood in your capillaries which in turn cool down the blood that is being pumped through your system at an increased rate.

Cooling down allows your body's system to slow down gradually from the increased level of work that exercise demands.

In addition to slowing down and walking through the last few minutes of your walking workout, it is also a good idea to go back through the stretching routine to make sure your muscles don't tighten up at all.

Simply return through the routine step by step, or to vary it, go through it from the last stretch to the first. You'll find that you'll feel better after your walk and the good feeling will last longer throughout the day.

Chapter Three

The Physiology of Walking

The activity of walking, pleasurable, relaxing walking—the kind of walking that you took on the beach that day—does not necessarily make walking an exercise.

An exercise means a physical activity that conditions the body through regular and continuous repetition of body movements over a specific time period. 'Conditions' is the important factor in this definition.

Exercise 'conditions' the body. For example, if you began an exercise routine in which you did five push-ups every morning for five weeks you will discover that by the end of the five weeks the five push-ups will become *easier*. Your body has been conditioned, it is now able to adapt to the particular stress of that activity.

The two main reasons for exercising are: to maintain/improve your health and to improve your level of physical fitness. The 'conditioning' component of exercise does this.

The way exercise conditions is through the repetition of the 'activity.' So it is the activity that contributes most directly to the person's long-term health.

For the purposes of cardiovascular fitness and body health a little bit of activity done properly is better than an excessive amount or inactivity. This statement is entirely consistent with my claim that effective exercise—exercise that maintains your health and improves your level of physical fitness—does not require pain.

What do I mean by being physically fit? Simply, I mean whatever level of fitness allows you to live a long, productive life that is emotionally and physically satisfying. Fitness doesn't necessarily make you happy, it simply ensures that you have the physical (and oftentimes, emotional) ability to appreciate and enjoy the things that do make you happy.

It just so happens that walking is an activity that can help you become physically fit and make you happy.

The following seven principles are paraphrased from many tests that have been conducted by scientists and researchers for the past 70 years. They explain how walking benefits your body physiologically.

Principle #1:

Your body will automatically adjust so that the energy required for you to cover the distance that you choose to walk will be the least amount of energy necessary to move your body over that distance.

What does this mean? Simply, it means that your body is a wondrous, wonderful organism that automatically works the least amount that it has to to get a job done. So if you walk a mile, your body will expend only the minimal amount of energy it would take to walk that mile; it will not burn the energy it would to walk, say, two miles.

This principle of energy conservation means that you always get your 'money's worth' from your body. It also means if you want to burn more energy in the form of calories, you have to work harder.

Principle #2:

This principle is a bit tricky if you become daunted in the face of mathematics. But bear with me because the principle is very interesting.

This interesting principle suggests that there is a constant relationship between the length of your stride and the rate of your stride (if you take into account differences in body height) according to the following formula:

Stride length/body height divided by step frequency/minute = .008

What does this formula mean? Basically it means that if you want to walk faster, you need to lengthen your strides and increase the frequency of your steps. That doesn't sound very complicated, does it? What is interesting about this formula is that making all these adjustments will still result in a constant number.

This means that we all find a natural stride, one that fits into this formula, as it turns out. If we alter any of the components of our natural stride—frequency or length—then we will require greater energy from our bodies, and therefore burn more calories.

Principle #3:

Adding weights to your body increases the amount of energy required to walk a given distance and adding this weight to your limbs has a greater effect than adding it to the trunk of your body.

So, if the goal is to increase your physical conditioning while walking—burn more calories, etc.—then you should create a greater burden for your body to move. And, this burden should be strategically placed.

For example, if you are a backpacker, you would use this principle to *lessen* your load. That is, by keeping the weight on your back as close to your trunk as possible, you reduce the energy required to carry that load.

If the weight of a backpacker's pack was distributed on his or her arms and legs, the energy required to carry it would be almost three times the energy required to carry that load.

Why? By placing the weight on moving limbs, you place it where it must be carried through a wider arc of movement.

Your limbs always work harder against greater resistance and weighting them creates greater resistance.

Principle #4:

The greater the slope you walk up (or down) the greater your energy expense (except going downhill on small grades).

What this principle expresses is something you know intuitively; walking uphill is harder than walking down a gentle slope or a flat surface.

The principle also states that walking *down* a steep grade is harder than walking down a gentle slope or a flat surface.

Walking uphill is more difficult, and therefore requires more energy and burns more calories because you are fighting some degree of gravity. When you walk downhill, gravity is 'helping' you.

However, when your downhill walk is very steep, you expend a good deal more energy than on a gentle downhill grade or on a flat surface because you have to constantly 'brake' yourself.

Principle #5:

Walking on uneven or difficult terrain increases the energy requirement in direct relationship to the difficulty of the terrain.

Example, your walk on the beach burned more calories than a walk of equal distance on a boardwalk. Why? Because the sand doesn't 'push' your feet up with each step. Therefore, you have to lift your legs higher with each step.

Lifting your legs higher forces your body to overcome gravitational forces—requiring you to expend greater energy.

Some studies indicate that weighted walking through loose sand requires an 80% increase in work to cover an equal distance.

Principle #6:

A distance of walking is 'worth' more in terms of metabolic expense if it is part of a series of distances walked rather than if it was walked discretely with longer than a ten minute rest interval in between.

Let's say you're going on a five mile walk. What this principle says is that walking those five miles will do you more good than walking one mile five times (with at least a ten minute interval between each mile).

Again, this principle makes sense intuitively. If you want to go a step further—test it. Check your pulse rate at the end of your first mile, then again after the second and third, etc. Your pulse rate should be increasing.

If you do the same thing after one mile, then rest ten minutes, walk another mile, count your pulse rate, rest ten minutes, etc., your pulse rate should be very close to the same each time you check it.

This principle suggests that a walker who chooses to walk long distances leisurely 'works' his or her body as much as someone who walks a shorter distance quickly.

Principle #7:

This principle states simply that you can 'add up' any or all of the previous principles to gain multiple benefits.

So if you speed up your walking over a greater distance on rough terrain with weights on your limbs you will be adding up the additional work your body does for each one of these tasks separately. Therefore, you can control the amount of work your body does while you walk and so control the number of calories it burns.

As I've stated in the context of several of these principles, many, if not all, of them are intuitively sound. You know what they state is correct. However scientists and researchers cannot rely on intuitive feelings to understand a phenomenon. Hours and hours of research for many years defined these principles.

Remember, I am talking about 'walking for fitness' when I discuss these principles. Fitness entails working your body, burning calories and conditioning it. But walking for fitness is different from most other fitness activities because even when you are benefiting yourself, it is still pleasurable.

You may never strap weights on your wrists or ankles to walk. You may never choose to walk up and down the steps of the local high school stadium. You may never choose to increase the speed of your walk. However, any of these things will increase the metabolic activity of your body, burn more calories and help condition it.

At the least, maybe try to vary the setting of your walks. This may bring you to a variety of terrains, hills and vistas. Walk and explore!

Use the principles to design your own walking routine. Vary your routine from week to week. Try different things. But always make sure your walks remain enjoyable and uniquely yours.

Physiological Testing

Are you in good shape? Fair shape? Poor shape? You might have an answer, but the way that you determine your answer is very important in determining how vigorously you should begin and continue the first few months of your walking/exercise routine.

The first thing you have to do in order to assess your 'shape' is to determine the degree of activity that defines your current lifestyle. Which of these categories describes you?

1. Inactive. Do you have a sit-down job and no regular activities?
2. Relatively Inactive. Is three to four hours of walking or standing per day usual? Do you have no regular organized physical activity during your leisure time?
3. Light Physical Activity. Are you occasionally involved in recreational activities such as weekend golf or tennis, jogging, swimming or cycling?
4. Moderate Physical Activity. Does your job regularly include lifting or stair climbing? Do you participate regularly in recreational or fitness activities such as jogging, swimming or cycling at least three times a week for 30 to 60 minutes each time?
5. Very Vigorous Physical Activity. Do you participate in extensive physical activity for 60 minutes or more at least four days per week?

Finding where you stand in the chart will help you to begin to assess your current physical fitness. However, in order to get a clearer sense of your fitness, you have to actually DO something. The something is a three-minute step test.

IF YOU HAVE ANY QUESTION IN YOUR MIND ABOUT TAKING IT CONSULT YOUR DOCTOR FIRST!

If not, it's easy to take and you'll have a clear picture of your cardiovascular response to exercise.

Step One. Taking Your Pulse

There are two places on your body most accessible for taking your pulse. The most commonly used is your wrist. In order to take your pulse at your wrist, place your fingers gently over the radial artery just inside your wrist bone.

If you have trouble finding your pulse, try jogging in place for 30 seconds. This should make it easier to locate. If you still can't locate your pulse at your wrist, try for the second place, near your Adam's apple.

To take your pulse here, insert your fingers gently into your neck at your Adam's apple and just beneath your jaw.

If you can't find your pulse in either of these two places, you can try pressing lightly on your temple or directly over your heart.

Now practice reading your pulse rate while resting. To do this you need only have a clock with a second hand. Count your pulse for thirty seconds and then multiply that number by 2. This is your heart rate per minute. For most people the resting pulse rate falls somewhere between 50 and 90 beats a minute.

Step Two. The Step Test

This test is a reliable way to test your heart's response to exercise. It is quick. It is easy. Perfect.

The way the step test works is by defining an activity (in this case stepping up and down a step) and a duration. 30 seconds after completing the test, you take your pulse for 30 seconds. That pulse rate will tell you the status of your fitness.

During the first minute of the test, your heart rate will increase rapidly and then start to level off. Then, when the test is over, the heart rate slows. The rate at which it slows after the activity is concluded is an important gauge of how fit you are.

The step test can be done alone but it is much easier with a friend. Remember, you must follow the test *exactly*.

First, you need a stair or stool eight inches high. You are going to step onto this height, one foot after another, up and down, for exactly three minutes.

You must follow the correct stepping cadence so practice before taking the test. You must step up and down twice within a five-second span, or 24 complete step-ups each minute. Each step-up has four footfalls. Your right foot returns to the floor and so does your left foot.

Up, up; down, down; up, up; down, down; each five second span. Each new sequence begins on a multiple of five seconds (5, 10, 15 and so on).

You must complete two full cycles every five seconds—no more, no less.

Once you understand and are comfortable with the cadence, time yourself or have someone else signal you to begin or stop.

Be precise and do the step test for exactly three minutes. The moment you stop, keep your eye on the second hand. Exactly 30 seconds after stopping, measure your pulse for 30 seconds. This is your heart rate recovery score.

Step 3. What does your Score Mean?

Here is a chart to measure and compare your heart rate recovery score:

	20-29 yrs	30-39 yrs number of	40-49 yrs beats	50+
MEN				
Excellent	34-36	35-38	37-39	37-40
Good	37-40	39-41	40-42	41-43
Average	41-42	42-43	43-44	44-45
Fair	43-47	44-47	45-49	46-49
Poor	48-59	48-59	50-60	50-62

WOMEN

Excellent	39-42	39-42	41-43	41-44
Good	43-44	43-45	44-45	45-47
Average	45-46	46-47	46-47	48-49
Fair	47-52	48-53	48-54	50-55
Poor	53-66	54-66	54-67	56-66

If you find that your step-test rating is significantly worse than your self-assessment (that is, if you assessed yourself as moderately active but your step-test rating was fair or poor) you should speak with your doctor. It may be that you are embarking on a level of physical activity that might not be healthy for you.

Burning your Fuel—Exercise and Calories

Food is the fuel that keeps your body going. Your body turns it into energy and cells. If you are inactive your body turns the food you eat into fat cells. If you are active, into muscle cells.

When you are active and your body is functioning efficiently, you 'burn' that fuel, use it up, so that you don't get overweight and so you have the energy to lead the life that you've chosen.

When we talk about burning up that fuel, we're talking about burning calories. Although we all have an intuitive sense of what that means, it is sometimes helpful to have a clearer understanding of how our body does this.

'Calorie' is a unit of energy. When we talk about calories, what we're really saying us: how much energy does a certain activity require of you? It is not unlike the mileage estimates of your car.

Your car gets a certain gas mileage. That mileage changes if conditions require your car to work harder—if you are driving uphill, have an air conditioner on, have a fully-loaded car, if the weather is hot, etc.

The harder your car works, the more gasoline (fuel) it burns.

The harder you work, the more fuel you burn.

If your car is finely tuned, you minimize the loss of fuel when it works harder. If you are in good condition, you are able to perform certain activities without working so hard (this goes back to our discussion of conditioning).

However, unlike our cars (where we like to save fuel) we should strive to burn calories efficiently. That is a major goal of any exercise program.

The most important measurement in any exercise is the amount of energy a particular activity forces the exerciser to expend. This measurement tells you how valuable the exercise is to you.

For instance, eating burns calories—but to many walking uphill with weights attached to your wrists and ankles burns a great deal more.

We will discuss calories a great deal more later in a chapter devoted to *nutrition*. For now all I'll say is that your body works on a balanced equation system. If you take in (eat) the same number of calories as you burn, your weight will remain the same. If you eat more than you burn, your body will convert the excess calories into fat cells. If you eat less than you burn, you will lose weight.

Each 'extra' 3500 calories equals about one pound of fat. It is up to you on which side of the equation those calories go. For instance if you diet or increase your energy output (exercise) by 3500 calories, you will lose a pound of fat.

Which means, if you reduce your food intake by only 100 calories a day and increase your exercise by 100 calories a day (by walking at a brisk pace for 20 minutes) you will be 'in the black' about 6000 calories in a month. If you figure that out, that adds up to a total of 21 pounds in a year. 100 calories is not very much. It would be simple to do better than that and still maintain a comfortable exercise program and a nutritious and healthy diet.

Chapter Four

These Shoes Were Made For Walking

One of the best things about walking is that the equipment that you need to begin, continue and master it is minimal. There is no need to invest tremendous numbers of dollars in fancy clothing, timing devices, nets, balls, bats, membership fees, etc.

However, one investment that should be made and should be made wisely is your shoes. These need not be expensive. They should just be the right shoes for you.

Take care of your feet and they will take care of you! And there is no better place to begin caring for your feet than in the shoes you put on them.

The most important features of a good walking shoe are comfort and support. Since comfort is primarily a function of how well a shoe fits and its 'upper body' and support has to do with the structural underpinning of the shoe, we will talk of them separately.

Comfort.

Comfort is a highly personalized feature. So bear in mind, you are an individual and have individual needs for comfort. These are general guidelines:

Measurements For Proper Shoe Fit

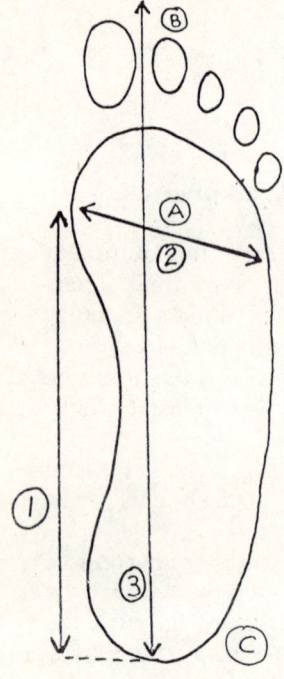

Shoe Fitting Tips

A When trying on a shoe be sure to check that there is enough space at the widest part of the foot. You should be able to wrinkle the upper shoe material across this area when standing.
B There should be 1/2 inch space ahead of the longest toe and the end of the shoe.
C The heel of the shoe should be as deep as possible to prevent slippage of the heel from the shoe.

1 Heel to ball of the foot at the widest point of forefoot.
2 Width at the widest point of the forefoot
3 Heel to toe length

1. The toe box must allow your toes to wiggle, spread out, expand. The toe box is a reinforcement that is built into the toe of the shoe to keep the original shape of the upper.

As a general rule, it is best to avoid narrow toe boxes. Only if you have a very narrow foot should you even consider a shoe with a narrow toe box.

If you choose a shoe that doesn't comfortably fit all parts of your foot then the price will be pain and blisters and most likely a loss of enthusiasm for walking. Don't risk that! If you err in sizing, err on the side for more room versus less.

As you walk, your foot 'flattens out.' That is, it tends to get longer and wider. They even become larger—due to the additional circulation of blood in your feet.

2. The shoe should be flexible—uppers and lowers.

Before you buy your shoe, push your finger into the uppers. It should feel reasonably soft.

The uppers is where individual preference truly takes hold. The question is whether the uppers should be leather, a combination of leather and fabric or just open-meshed fabric.

The advantage to the nylon mesh is that it allows your foot to 'breathe.' The more air you can get to your foot while you're walking, the drier it will be, the less likely to blister and burn.

However, proponents of all-leather uppers claim that the additional support that leather (not the soft, soft, leather, but somewhat stiff leather) provides is very beneficial.

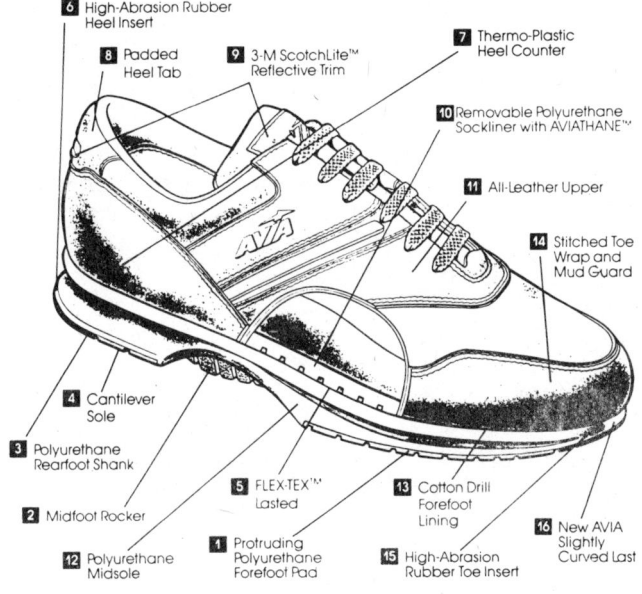

Again, these are individual preferences. Although support is an important factor, combination uppers of nylon mesh and leather also provide support. Experiment with both kinds and find the one that is most comfortable for you.

One thing that everyone agrees on in regards to uppers is that you must pay close attention to how well they are constructed. Make sure the uppers are stitched together well. Any roughly finished seams will cause blisters. Make sure you feel the inside of the uppers carefully.

3. The shoe should be light weight.

Construction

This is the actual support structure of the shoe itself.

A. There should be a firm heel counter. This keeps your foot in line. When you walk, there is a tendency to pronate, to turn your foot out. When this happens, your arch drops a little. This negates the foot's natural shock-absorbing mechanism.

Excessive pronation causes the arch to drop more, causing soreness, fatigue and strain.

One of the major differences between running and walking shoes is that in a good walking shoe the heel counter is carried far forward, providing greater protection from pronation.

B. There should be a cushioned sole.

The best walking shoes combine multidensity materials on the inside of the shoe to cushion the foot—soft material at the top and more resilient material on the bottom.

Remember, the shape of the cushioned sole is determined by *averages* in human anatomy and each shoe manufacturer develops this differently. Find one that feels good to you.

C. Outersoles.

The outersole should feel reasonably soft. It must be of a durable material and should have 'bounce.' The best way to determine the bounce of the outersole is to take the shoe and strike it against a hard surface.

The outersole should have a 'rocker' profile. This includes a sweep at the toe to encourage the roll of the foot and to aid in the natural walking motion.

A heel height of between three-eighths and five-eighths of an inch will help reduce stretching of the Achilles tendon and place the foot at the proper forward pitch while walking.

Foot Care

Take care of your feet! They are the difference between a long life of enjoyable walking and a frustrating and quick end to the whole process. Tired, burning, chafed, blistered feet do not a walker make. Fortunately, basic and simple foot care can almost entirely eliminate all of the above discomforts.

The most important aspect of keeping you feet healthy is to keep them dry! One way to do this is to 'air them out' regularly.

Another thing to be very careful about is SOCKS. Socks should be absorbent. Because of this, cotton socks (the higher the percentage of cotton, the better) are preferable. Your socks do not need to be thick. Thickness is a matter of preference more than need.

Each one of your feet gives off about a cup of perspiration a day. The majority of that wetness gets ventilated through the top rim of the shoe. The rest goes into the shoe damaging the shoes unless you have absorbent socks. Moisture makes the foot itchy and rashy and creates a perfect breeding ground for blisters.

Toenails should be trimmed. They needn't be very short but if they are too long, they can cause problems as your foot expands while you walk.

Sometimes it is a good idea to rub petroleum jelly on your feet to prevent blisters. Although this feels very peculiar at first, after you put your socks on and begin to walk you'll forget about it.

More elaborate foot care (and foot pampering) is a highly individual preference. Some walkers suggest massages or baths after walking.

Washing *is* very important. Clean, dry feet are the goal.

Additional suggestions include alternating hot/cold foot baths after walking. The alternating warm and cold soaks serve to exercise the arteries, veins and lymph channels and thus help to remove excess fluid from the foot, ankle and legs.

Fill one basin with ice-cold water and another with water that is as hot as you can bear it. Put your feet in the ice water for one minute, then immediately put them in the hot basin for one minute. Repeat five to ten times, then dry your feet with a rough towel.

To massage your feet, follow these steps:

Work your closed fist into the sole of your foot in a circular motion. Then work your thumbs into the heel and arch area. Squeeze each foot with both hands, sliding your thumbs down to the edge of the sole. Then hold each toe, one at a time, with your thumb and index finger, gently pulling and allowing your fingers to slide off.

Foot care is simple and easy. Don't neglect this. Taking proper care of your feet will ensure an enjoyable walking experience.

Chapter Five

Walking Health

Now, after you've gotten a good pair of shoes, you've probably begun to map out in your mind the routes you would choose to walk. You can picture the shady, tree-lined avenue, or the vast green stretches of the golf course, or the bright music that you'll be able to hear over the mall's sound system.

In other words, you're really ready to begin. The only question that remains is: How to start?

The question may sound silly, especially after all I've been saying about walking. But like anything else, you have to take the first step.

I had one friend, call her Annie, whom I'd finally convinced to give walking a try. She got very enthused with the idea, went out and bought good shoes, a nice warm-up suit, even a small radio with the lightweight headphones so she could listen to some music while she walked around the local golf course.

I cautioned her not to have the music on too loudly. If there were any dangers that she would have to hear—like a car coming, a train, anything—the radio should be her friend, not her enemy. But other than that, I was pleased with her readiness. I wished her good luck and told her to call me and let me know how it was going.

After two weeks, I hadn't heard from Annie so I gave her a call. She sounded a little embarrassed to hear from me so I asked her what the matter was.

"I haven't started yet," she admitted glumly.

I asked her, "why not?"

"Well," she said, "I kept getting tripped up by a lot of little stupid things."

"Like what?" I wanted to know.

"Well, for instance, do I drive to the golf course or walk there?

I mean, I feel so silly driving five blocks to exercise. It seems I should walk there and walk back too.

"And another thing, I was walking around the house the other day and I noticed that my toes don't point out straight when I walk like they're supposed to.

"And I can't figure out how to get these damn batteries in my radio."

It seemed to me that Annie was suffering from the new walker's version of 'stage fright.' Any time you begin a new activity you experience a certain degree of apprehension. That's true whether it's your first day of school, your wedding day or beginning a walking routine.

My advice to Annie? Forget the radio at first. I'll help with the batteries if after a week she decided she wanted it. Drive in the beginning. Annie had carefully planned out her walking route. As it turned out, after a couple of months, she increased the distance she walked and in the process included the walk to and from her house.

The only point that Annie had made that really concerned me (except for the fact that she was bothered by the other things) was the self-consciousness about her toes pointing outward.

The notion that when we walk our toes must point straight forward is a problematic one. Like all artificial notions of the 'way things are supposed to be' it is not really true and, to a certain extent, is damaging.

Only about ten percent of the population (in fact, of any population—studies have shown this to be the case with populations in Africa where they wear no shoes as well as populations in cities like New York and Los Angeles) really walk with their toes pointed straight ahead. For most people, they toe out at between 5 and 15 degrees.

When I asked Annie how much her toes 'pointed out' she told me, and I assured her her walking style was normal and she had nothing to worry about. If her toes did point out more than fifteen degrees then I would have advised seeing a podiatrist.

There are a million reasons not to do anything. Getting started means overcoming those 'obstacles' that we put in our own way. Remember, in the case of walking, walking is enjoyable AND beneficial. Don't let obstacles or 'stage fright' hinder you!

I have made the point over and over that walking is natural and easy. It does not require any special sports skills or talents. There are, however, certain techniques that will allow you to get the greatest amount of benefit from your walking. In addition, I will give you an idea how to design a program that is comfortable for you that will allow you to vary your walking while at the same time increasing your stamina, strengthening your heart and burning those calories.

The first time you do these techniques they will most likely feel strange to you. That is primarily because few of us are conscious of the components of any of the activities we perform. In any case, within a couple of days these techniques will become second nature to you and you will find it difficult to remember a time when they seemed foreign. Also, you will adapt the techniques so that they are comfortable for you. You *do not* have to adapt to a technique. The technique has to adapt to you!

The first 'technique' is the starting position. Basically, this requires that you hold proper posture. Proper posture does a number of things for you. Primarily, it allows you to breathe more freely and more fully by expanding your chest cavity and straightening your windpipe. So, here goes!

Stand with your feet parallel and a bit less than shoulder width apart. Hold your head up. Keep your shoulders back but try not to tense them or your back muscles. Straighten your back.

One of the tricks to good posture while you walk is where you focus your eyes. They guide you in many essential ways. Focus your eyes forward and look out about fifteen to twenty feet ahead of you.

Hang your hands at your side with your palms turned inward and your fingers stretched out and relaxed. Notice, I said 'hang' your hands. Don't tense them but really do let them hang loosely by your side.

Your knees should be slightly bent. Hold your stomach in and tuck your buttocks in.

Now, if after reading this you think that just getting yourself aligned to walk is enough exercise for one day, don't be discouraged. All these things do is put your body in an efficient position to benefit you. And, you should be relaxed. Good posture in anything should never be anything but *relaxing*. Good posture does not require a military stance. Maintaining good posture while you walk will strengthen those muscles used for maintaining good posture.

It is a happy and never ending cycle.

One of the things that distinguishes walkers from runners (besides the smile on their faces) is that a walker *always* maintains ground contact with one or both feet. This brings us to our second technique, bringing your leg through.

From the basic position described in the first technique, swing your left (or right if it's more comfortable) forward five to twelve inches off the ground. Keep your toes pointed in the direction of travel.

Now, in swinging your leg forward, raise your heel first and then push off with your toes. Keep your rear leg straight with the toes pointed in the direction of travel.

When your forward foot hits the ground, straighten it. Start your rear leg swing by pushing off with your toes. Begin to shift your arms so that your forward arm (which should be on the opposite side of your body to your forward leg) swings back and your back arm swings forward.

One thing to be aware of, don't straighten your leg completely until your foot makes contact with the ground. You should hit the ground with your heel, then 'roll' your foot forward to your toes and continue the motion.

You are walking! And to think, we thought toddlers mastered this at two years of age.

The only other technique that is important to point out has to do with breathing. The most efficient way to breathe while you walk is to synchronize your breathing with your swinging arms. Depending on which leg you take forward first (and therefore, which arm you swing back first) breathe in with your first leg swing, breathe out as you bring your back leg forward. Or breathe in with your first arm going back and out when your bring the opposite arm forward.

That's all you need to know about technique. And if it seemed a bit wordy, remember—one walk is worth a thousand words (to paraphrase an old saying). Get out and walk! The perfecting of the techniques and the way you adapt them to your body will come.

Now that you've gotten over your 'stage fright' and begun to incorporate these simple techniques, you'll probably find yourself wanting to increase your distances or to walk faster—almost anything to take advantage of your increased stamina and joy in walking.

As with any exercise, especially if you haven't been active for awhile, you should start out slowly, finding your most comfortable level of exercise. Maintain that for a couple of weeks and then begin to build on it.

In the beginning you should plan on walking short distances with great frequency (seven times a week). This accomplishes two things. The first is that it develops a routine and a discipline. The second is that it brings you into shape relatively quickly.

For example, during the first few weeks, try walking every day for a short distance. Begin with no more than one eighth of a mile (if you're walking on a track, this equals one half of one time around). If you do this every day of the week your cumulative total distance will equal seven eighths of a mile. In addition, you will burn about 100 calories a day.

Keep in mind that you should set for yourself some realistic (emphasis should be on realistic) goal for yourself. Perhaps a goal of two miles walked without a rest is a reasonable goal for the first couple of months.

Over the course of the next five or six weeks, increase the distance you walk by a half a lap. If you're not walking on a track you might want to use a pedometer, or if you're walking along a lane or boulevard, try driving along your route and assign distances to certain landmarks like trees or corners or something.

As your walking distance increases (after six or seven weeks you will be up to your goal of two miles) you might want to vary your routine. Walk longer distances but only three to four times a week. *Do not* get into the runner's trap of exercising even when it's not enjoyable because you are wedded to some silly routine. Remember, walking has to be enjoyable. Don't make it anything less. If you're not up to it one day—take the day off. You have my permission!

Our goal is a long term, life-style exercise program. For your program to be successful it must adapt to your life more than you adapt to its demands.

Returning to your routine—and keeping in mind it is your routine, you are not its victim—continue to increase your distance by a quarter to a half mile per week. By the end of three or four months, you will be walking as much as four to five miles a day at least three times a week. In the process you will be healthier, you will feel healthier and you will be using at least 1200 calories a week. That, with a sensible nutrition plan (which we will discuss later) will make you lose those inches you've wanted to lose, tighten those inches you want to keep and generally make you feel like a million.

If you are able and if you have the mind to, you can continue to increase your distance at approximately the same rate that you have in the beginning. Within a year, if you choose, you can easily be walking upwards of ten miles on each walking outing. To get the maximum benefits, you should walk at least three times a week. If you do walk that distance three times a week you will burn upwards of 3000 calories a week and you will be in the upper echelon of walkers.

Now, your goals needn't be thirty miles a week. Or even ten. What is important is that you *walk*. Regularly and for a distance that allows your body to reap the benefits of your activity.

You can do it. You want to. Just enjoy it. Feel good. Smile.

In a year you will be a year older whether you decide to walk or not. You might as well use the year and be a year older, a year happier, a year healthier and a year wiser.

I know that it is easier to read a few pages in a book than it is to walk to develop a routine that will satisfy you for a year, then two years, then your whole life. I don't mean to minimize the fact that you will be doing the work. I only want to emphasize that it needn't feel like work and that *you have to take that first step.*

When I finally got Annie back on track I was pleased and I knew she was. A few days later, the phone rang.

"Hello?"

"Hi, it's me, Annie."

"Hello, Annie. How are you?"

"You're going to think I'm very silly," she started.

"Oh, I doubt that," I assured her.

"Now, I know you're going to think I'm just an airhead, albeit an older version."

"I could never think that about you," I said. "What's the problem?"

"I don't know what to wear."

I started to tell her that she shouldn't worry about things like that, but then I stopped. Annie's question was an important one. My first instinct was to say to wear anything that was comfortable and to a certain extent that would have been correct. Walking wear is really any piece of clothing that will help you walk in whatever terrain or weather conditions that you might encounter on your walk. But I realized that that was much too general an observation to help Annie.

The clothing should be lighter than most clothing because a great deal of heat is generated when you walk. Also, your clothing should be layered on cooler days. This allows the various layers of clothing to 'trap' the warm air coming from your body and to actually insulate you from the cooler air around you. Also, layered clothing can be removed in stages as you warm up along your walk. Clothing that is comfortable the first mile might be too much by the fifth. And of course, whatever you wear, it must be loose enough to allow your arms and legs to swing in full arcs.

However, as correct as all of the above is, it doesn't give the full picture for a walker in the 1990's.

Headgear and Sunglasses

Sunglasses and some kind of head covering serve the vital function of protecting your head and eyes from the sun's rays, if you're going to be walking for any length of time, certainly if you'll be walking in the sun. Continuous exposure to the sun, even a relatively weak sun, can cause headaches, dizziness, and temporary difficulty with vision. The sun's effect is even more powerful on the eyes when it is reflected up from surfaces below you such as asphalt, water and even some dirt roads.

Don't take chances with the sun. It is a wonderful ally but a powerful enemy. Don't cross it!

Wear sunglasses that block out the sun's harshest rays. There are many on the market. Some people seem to feel the 'mirrored' lenses afford them the greatest protection. You will have to judge for yourself. If you wear prescription glasses, you can have glasses made up in dark lenses to protect your eyes. Explore the possibilities.

Wear a hat! In warm weather, your walking hat should have a rounded crown that creates an air pocket above your head. This allows air to pass between your head and the top of your hat. There are also hats whose crowns are made from a mesh material to allow air passage. These are also very good. Your hat should have a visor to help shield your eyes.

In cooler weather, your walking hat should be of knitted material like wool. This holds your body's heat to your head. (A tremendous amount of your body's heat is lost from your head and your extremities. This is why, in cold weather, it is very important to wear hat, gloves, and good socks and shoes.)

Inadequate headgear and sunglasses can cut short your walking outing as well as leave you with a headache and miserable feeling.

Upper Body Wear

Again, the layered approach is the most successful one of if you are walking in cool or cold weather. It is a good idea to begin with two, three or even four layers of warm clothing which can be peeled off as you warm up. If it's very cold, a wool scarf is a good idea to have along. It can shield exposed areas of the face and neck and make your walk much more pleasant.

If it is windy, a wind jacket and perhaps wind pants will serve you well.

When planning your layers, you should begin with a longsleeved or short sleeved T-shirt, then a lightweight sweater or sweatshirt, and then a heavier sweater or jacket.

Some people prefer turtle neck T-shirts, others complain that they trap too much body heat and cause them to sweat more than they need to or feel comfortable doing. Try both ways and see which is most comfortable for you.

If you are walking on a wet and rainy day (which does have a wonderful appeal), beware not to remain wet for too long. If your clothing becomes soaked through to the skin, your body may cool down, resulting in a dangerous situation called hypothermia.

Hypothermia is a condition in which the body's core temperature drops drastically and the system in unable to regain its natural temperature. Hypothermia is potentially fatal. It is not a condition to take lightly.

For most walkers, there is little danger of getting into this situation. But if you are a hiker or are a great distance from your destination and the rain is heavy, you must beware.

When walking in the rain, try to keep your clothes (especially those layers against the skin) dry. This requires frequent changes. Also, choose the material of your clothing well. Wool is a good, traditional choice because it breathes well and absorbs moisture in a way that doesn't let the body cool down too much so you won't freeze if you get too wet. (You will still be very uncomfortable, however.)

There are new synthetic materials on the market such as "Thinsulate" and "Gore-Tex", which make outdoor clothing lighter and protective against the elements. They do this by creating a weave that is too small to allow water in but large enough to allow the heat vapor (steam) from your body to escape. To fully understand this, you need to understand chemistry and physics. To enjoy a walk on a rainy and cold day, you need only know that it works.

Unfortunately, outfits made of these synthetic materials are fairly expensive so you'll have to evaluate your own needs and capabilities in choosing whether or not to use them.

A poncho may be a good compromise for the 'rain-walker.' Although the rubber or plastic material doesn't breathe well, it is loose enough by design that air flows in and around it. It also allows for enough room so you can carry a pack, which I'll discuss later.

However, if you're walking along the beach in the nice warm sun (or anywhere for that matter if it's warm) then upper body requirements are much easier to fulfill.

A T-shirt or a shirt with straps is the best because it allows for great upper body freedom. Clothing should be seamless or have outside seams so they avoid rubbing the skin.

For maximum flexibility and speed, bare-chested walking (or for women, a halter top) may be best of all. But if you choose to walk with your skin exposed use PLENTY of suntan or sunblock lotion.

If the weather permits it, walking shorts are the best for your legs. If the weather is cool, the same rule applies to the legs as to the upper body—layers. But avoid tight-fitting restrictive pants.

If you are walking a great distance or if you are walking somewhere where certain amenities are lacking, you might want to consider carrying such things along. This will require that you carry a back or belt pack. Depending on the amount of things you will carry, you can decide on the one for you. But be sure to check to make sure the straps are comfortable and balanced well. And, don't carry too much. There's no point in weighing yourself down for no reason.

And finally, you might want to consider a walking stick or staff. Besides making your walk an enjoyable affair that allows you to imagine yourself in the movies, a stick or staff can serve several useful functions. One, if there are unfriendly dogs about, it can provide a source of security and protection. Two, some sticks and staffs have built-in umbrellas that will protect you against unforeseen weather changes. And finally, it is a wonderful thing to lean on to just catch your wind and look at the wonderful world around you.

Anyway, I ended up telling Annie that she wasn't being silly at all.

Chapter Six

Nutrition

It seems like a long journey already from the time I was walking alongside you in the sand. During that time (and these pages) I've tried to convince you to walk. But not just because walking is so beneficial, which it is, but because I believe that walking is the single most perfect exercise by which you can make your life more full, more healthy and more enriching.

I know it seems like a lot. But as I've tried to show you, it's true.

However, as much as what you do in the form of exercise, as much as your exercise routine can determine good health, weight loss, feelings of well-being, etc., one component to a healthy lifestyle that might be even more important (although, of course, it should be in conjunction with an exercise program like walking) is a diet. Nutrition. What you eat.

You've heard the phrase, "You are what you eat." Take it to heart. As one researcher has pointed out, although we live in a tremendous advanced terminological age, when we can fly anywhere at a moment's notice, see and speak with anyone almost anywhere, can call up entire encyclopedias of knowledge with the push of a computer key, we still live in the body of a cave person.

What this means is that our nutritional requirements haven't changed significanctly in thousands of years—but, the way we utilize our food and how effectively we use our body's chemistry have changed dramatically.

During the Stone Age, when food was scarce, it was important that almost everything eaten got 'stored' in the body to be used at a later date when food wasn't available. Well, the way food gets stored is by being turned into fat.

For most of us, food scarcity is not a problem. In fact, too much food is. And 'fat' has become a dirty word. That is why diet and nutrition is such an important element in our overall health. We have to eat well to be well.

Speaking of nutrition, let us share with you first of all the single most important nutrient that you will ever need to enhance your athletic ability, your performance and your endurance.

Are you ready? Okay. Water.

Water?

Yes, water.

Water is the seemingly magical substance that has helped to improve the energy, stamina, performance of many world renowned athletes. It can do the same for you whether you choose to walk one mile or ten.

Every chemical reaction in you body, including energy production, takes place in a watery environment. If your blood, muscles, or other organs do not get optimal amounts of water they will not function at anything close to their peak performance levels.

Scientific studies have shown that when you lose as little as two pounds of water during exercise (and that is not very much—you don't usually notice the amount of water you lose because it evaporates so quickly) your ability to perform hard work can drop by 15%.

A seven pound water loss, which is not extraordinary if you're walking on a warm, humid day a long distance, can decrease work ability by as much as 10%!

For many of us, the threat of dehydration doesn't seem real because we have too much faith in our body's warning mechanism as it regards drinking. We wait until we are thirsty before drinking. This is waiting too long.

Many people in good shape can tolerate a water loss of up to 5% of their body weight before their thirst makes them drink. But by then the debilitating effects of dehydration already have occurred.

Thirst does not keep up with water loss!

Don't let this lag keep you from drinking enough water to keep your body hydrated. Fatigue, cramping....many of the unpleasant and even dangerous aspects of exercise can be avoided simply by making sure that you drink enough.

And drink water. Water. Don't waste your time or money with soft drinks or even drinks that are touted on commercials as 'sports drinks.' These drinks contain much too much sodium and sugar and they stay in your stomach too long to benefit your athletic performance. Pure water leaves the stomach and enters the bloodstream much faster, thereby benefiting you more.

NUTRITION

I am not advocating a specific diet program. Rather, what I would like to do is to give you an overview of the nutritional benefit of eating well.

We all know that we should be eating balanced meals, cutting down on our caloric intake and staying away from fats. The question is, why? We know caloric intake increases our weight. But fat consumption might only be a vaguely understood danger. And it is in understanding fat consumption and its dangers that we can truly understand the benefits of nutrition, certainly as it relates to a healthy cardiovascular system.

In order to understand this, I have to delve a bit deeper into the way your body works and specifically, into the chemical structure of blood. In many ways, your blood chemistry is as individual as your fingerprints.

Your blood chemistry is concerned not so much with the blood itself (the red platelets, the white ones, etc.) but with other substances that reside within your veins and arteries helping or hindering the motions or circulation of your blood throughout your body.

There are five vital values, your total cholesterol level, high-density lipoprotein (HDL) cholesterol, glucose (blood sugar), triglycerides (blood fats) and uric acid. In order to get these values so that you know the level of your own 'blood health' you should have a simple, inexpensive laboratory test called a blood chemistry profile. Before taking the test, you should not eat or drink anything (except water) for 12 hours before you have the profile taken.

Now, let's go back to the five vital values. What are they and where do they come from?

CHOLESTEROL

We've all heard a great deal about cholesterol. It has been characterized as the great enemy of the times. However, things are not that simple. Cholesterol is present in foods of animal origin. It is also manufactured by the body from everything we eat. A certain amount of cholesterol is vital to our health and well-being. As an example, if we had no cholesterol, we would have no sex hormones.

The problem with cholesterol comes about when there is too much in our veins and arteries. This comes about because our bodies are 'water based.' Cholesterol is fat soluble (which means basically that it doesn't mix with water. It's like those globules that float to the top of the frying pan when you soak it in water after frying sausages or something). Because it is fat soluble, it doesn't mix well with the blood. Therefore our bodies must package cholesterol in water-soluble 'containers' called lipoproteins, in order to transport it through the blood supply.

There are four different lipoproteins and all but one contribute to 'clogging' your arteries, impeding your blood flow and raising the risk of stroke or heart attack. However the fourth, called high-density lipoprotein (HDL) is actually beneficial to you. Studies indicate that the higher your HDL level the lower your risk of heart attack. The more of your total cholesterol that is carried in HDL protein containers, the less cholesterol is available to clog your arteries. Therefore in nutrition, the goal is to keep HDL cholesterol high and total cholesterol low.

GLUCOSE

Your blood sugar determines your enemy levels, especially during exercise and stress. For reasons not yet fully understood, low blood sugar can even affect your emotions, making you irritable and easily upset.

When the concentration of blood glucose falls below the normal fasting level (usually below 50 milligrams for every 3.5 ounces of blood), a condition called hypoglycemia results.

Since sugar is the brain's favorite food (and the brain cannot store sugar the way the muscles can), severe hypoglycemia literally starves the brain. Poor sports performance, even unconsciousness, may result.

On the other hand, when blood sugar levels are too high, the kidneys begin to transfer some of the excess sugar to the urine. This can signal the first signs of diabetes mellitus.

Although blood sugar (glucose) shares the same name as the sugar you're familiar with from your cupboard or candy bars, it is not the same thing. There are many types of sugars (although all share the chemical ending -ose). For an example, when reading the ingredients some time, notice the sucrose, fructose, etc. They are sugars and not always good for you.

Sugars, the enemy packets, are created by the body by breaking down carbohydrates, especially complex carbohydrates. A spoonful of sugar might make the medicine go down but it is not necessary to maintain good blood sugar levels. Eating complex carbohydrates is.

TRIGLYCERIDES

These are fats that can be found in ordinary foods as well as in our bodies. Triglycerides are the fats we store around our bellies, thighs and anyplace else on our bodies that bulge with nonmuscular weight.

The level of blood triglycerides reveals many things about the foods you eat and how well your body handles these foods. Abnormally high levels may deprive your working muscles of vital oxygen—resulting in diminished stamina and endurance.

An elevated triglyceride reading, like elevated cholesterol, may even increase your risk of cardiovascular disease.

URIC ACID

This is a toxic substance that is actually manufactured by the body in small amounts from compounds called purines, which are to be found in ordinary foods such as meat, seafood and peas. Normally, the kidneys help to excrete excessive uric acid quite well.

Uric acid is a vital blood value to check, however, because when uric acid blood levels increase beyond 6.5 milligrams for every 3.5 ounces of blood, salts of uric acid (sodium urate) may lodge in joints, causing swelling, inflammation, pain and damage. This condition is actually an arthritic condition called gout. Excessive uric acid can also form kidney stones, a very painful and health-threatening condition.

Something to be aware of: Whenever you attempt to lose weight through *any* type of diet and/or exercise plan, you should first consult with a physician, because weight loss may temporarily elevate uric acid levels. The temporary rise in the uric acid level is easily controlled by medications such as allopurinol and probenecid.

As I noted above, I am not advocating a specific diet or nutritional plan. I *do* advocate sensible eating, limiting caloric intake, getting lots of fresh foods such as fruits and vegetables, limiting your consumption of animal fats and getting *creative* with your meals. However, these are all personal choices (much like the choice of your walking setting—beach or shopping mall).

I will, however offer very general guidelines about the percentages of which food should make up your diet. Which foods you choose to eat, when and how is left to your best judgment.

However, before I do, let us just note that when taking your blood chemistry profile remember that interpreting the results can be a bit misleading. In general 'normal' ranges in the United States tend to be a bit high. Try and keep well down in those ranges.

Now about those percentages...

Complex carbohydrates (starches such as pasta, potatoes, breads, grains) should make up the bulk of your diet, somewhere from 60—80%. And remember, a potato has almost no calories (less than an apple) however, drowning it in butter and sour cream and salt increases the amount of calories and reduces the 'healthiness' of the meal. The same goes for pastas like spaghetti. It's the topping that'll kill you.

Simple carbohydrates (sweets) should make up only 5 — 10% of your daily diet. Still, that's a nice treat. There's no reason to deprive yourself of treats. Just limit them.

Protein (animal or vegetable). Keep to around 10 — 15% of

your daily calories. Proteins have gotten an underserved 'good rap' lately. Everyone talks about high protein diets, etc. Unfortunately, the body doesn't utilize proteins as efficiently as it does carbohydrates. Instead, there is the tendency to turn it into fat.

Fats (animal or vegetable) should make up between 5 — 20% of your caloric intake.

As you get into your walking program and as you become more and more aware of your general health and diet, you will find yourself eating the lower percentages of sweets and fats and probably increasing the percentage of complex carbohydrates.

CARBOHYDRATES
60-80% of your daily kilocalories

- Cereals
- Whole grain breads
- Pasta
- Brown rice
- Potatoes
- Whole grain pancakes
- Vegetables (steamed or raw)
- Fruit juices
- Dried fruits
- Fresh fruits

FATS AND OILS
5-20% of your daily kilocalories

Only 1 portion (one tablespoon total fats and oils) is permitted per day from the following lists

- Olive oil
- Any vegetable oil (corn, sesame, safflower)
- Margarine, low calorie type
- Margarine regular type
- Mayonnaise
- Avoid peanut oil, butter, and lard

PROTEINS
10-15% of your daily kilocalories

Skim milk
Nonfat dry milk
Low fat, part skim cheeses
Grated parmesan or romano cheese
Low fat cottage cheese
Low fat yogurt
Meats: poultry, fish, shellfish, veal, lean cut beef, pork, lamb, venison, duck
Legumes: beans, peas, lentils
Nuts and seeds

Just remember, diet, like a really beneficial exercise program, isn't just a question of which foods you have for breakfast or lunch. To be effective and to have a long term and long lasting beneficial affect, your diet and exercise program must represent a reorientation in lifestyle.

That is why it's important to choose a diet and exercise (like walking) that isn't radically different from your 'normal' lifestyle. Radical changes are difficult for most people and extremely difficult to maintain over the course of years.

You have to enjoy your diet and lifestyle. ENJOY YOUR LIFE and all the facets of it. That's the goal. Good health is a primary component of that goal. But the practices that help you achieve good health and maintain it must be enjoyable in their own right.

The logic of punishing yourself in pursuit of an 'enjoyable' goal escapes me.

MINERALS

Minerals are basic chemicals that can be found in the soil. Plants draw minerals up from the soil, animals get minerals when they eat the plants. Man receives the minerals when he eats either plants or animals. This is the basic outline of the food cycle.

Without minerals nerve impulses couldn't be conducted through the body. These impulses control everything from heartbeat to the contraction of muscles. Minerals also control the amount of water your body can hold and how it is stored.

Fruits, vegetables, grains and nuts are particularly rich sources of minerals. By eating these things, we incorporate minerals into our bodies.

Each mineral performs specific functions within the body. For example, we are all beginning to hear a lot about calcium in regards to osteoporosis, a condition that affects many older women. This condition is the loss of bone density. Calcium is a mineral that makes bones and teeth hard by increasing the density of the bones. Salt, a mineral that to a certain degree has been maligned because of our tremendous overuse of it, is vital to the way the body regulates the body's water supply, where it is distributed in the body and how. Magnesium regulates muscle contraction and the conversion process by which carbohydrates are converted to energy.

Other minerals are necessary because of the way that they contribute to the way in which other body functions are maintained. Some minerals form chemicals that regulate body processes. For example, iodine in thyroid hormone, iron in hemoglobin, zinc in insulin, cobalt in vitamin B12, and sulfur in thiamin and biotin.

Below is a chart that outlines the minerals that the body needs and in which general amount (large, or trace).

Minerals the Body Needs in Large Amounts

Sodium	Magnesium
Potassium	Calcium

Minerals The Body Needs in Trace Amounts

Aluminum	Iodine	Selenium
Boron	Iron	Tin
Chromium	Manganese	Vanadium
Cobalt	Molybdenum	Zinc
Copper	Nickel	

Mineral	Source	Recommended daily allowances
Calcium	milk and leafy green vegetables	250 mgm.
Phosphate	milk	750 mgm.
Magnesium	nuts, dark bread, beer, and green leafy vegetables	200 mgm.
Potassium	fruits and vegetables	not est.
Manganese	beans	5 mgm.
Iron	raisins	15 mgm.
Copper	beans	2 mgm.
Cobalt	spinach	.1 mgm
Iodine	fruits and vegetables grown in coastal areas	.15 mgm.
Sulfur	beans	not est.
Zinc	whole wheat bread	15 mgm.
Fluorine	apples	not est.
Selenium	fruits and vegetables depending on the selenium contents of the soil in which whey are grown	.02 mgm.
Chromium	fruits and vegetables depending on the chromium content of the soil in which whey are grown	1 mgm.
Molybdenum	fruits and vegetables depending on the molybdenum content of the soil in which whey are grown	.1 mgm.
Sodium	meat and milk products	200 mgm.

SODIUM (SALT)

Of all the minerals that are in the body's blood stream, salt is the one present in the largest quantity. Every active person needs salt. When the body runs low of salt it becomes dehydrated, muscles begin to cramp and a general malaise takes over.

However, in spite of the fact that salt is an absolute necessity *add as little as possible (or none) to your food when you cook or eat!*

If these two statements appear to be contradictory, they are not. As I noted above, Americans consume much too much salt. All the salt that your body requires can be found in the foods you eat (indeed, much more that your body requires). Meat, fish, chicken, grains and nuts are all loaded with salt. All milk products (save those advertised as low in salt) are high in salt content. All margarines (again, except those advertised as being low in salt). Olives are high in salt. Many bran, rye, wheat and corn products. Anything that tastes salty is. Almost all canned foods have added salt. Ketchup, potato chips, french fries, popcorn—you name it. There is more than enough salt in everything you eat.

Just as too little salt creates a dangerous situation in your body so too does too much salt. Too much salt dehydrates. In low levels, salt helps your body retain water. But excess salt increases urination. Also, by drawing more fluid out of the body it contributes to heat exhaustion and heatstroke.

Excess salt increases the body's loss of potassium through the kidneys. This could lead to chronic fatigue.

And, of course, the dangers of excess that many of us are familiar with—too much in the blood can cause clotting which can lead to heart attack, stroke, kidney failure, blindness, loss of a limb or death.

POTASSIUM

If you are in reasonably good shape and have maintained a regular exercise routine for some time and then find that you are feeling weak and tired for extended periods of time you may be suffering from a deficiency in the minerals that reside inside the muscle cells. Of the two, potassium deficiency is the more common.

Potassium deficiency is particularly prevalent in older people and those who take diuretics or who have diarrhea.

Part of the reason for this is that potassium is water soluble and washes out of the system easily with sweat or water loss (as in people with diarrhea or who take diuretics.)

Unfortunately, the body possesses no built-in warning system to warn you of a potassium shortage. For some things, there is such a system. When you are thirsty, your body is telling you you need water. When you are low on salt, your body craves salty foods. But when your potassium level drops, you just feel tired, weak and irritable and probably blame it on a million different things.

A simple blood test can show potassium deficiency. Rejuvenation can come about by ingesting large quantities of foods rich in potassium.

Potassium loss increases with increased exercise. Thus, when you are in your exercise routine, be sure to replenish your potassium supply.

MAGNESIUM

Magnesium is involved in the process of muscle contraction and the regulation of the process of conversion of carbohydrates to energy. Low levels of magnesium in the muscle cells result in muscle cramps and chronic fatigue.

Magnesium is lost through sweat and stools. Magnesium loss increases with increased activity. In order to avoid a magnesium deficiency, eat lots of dark bread, nuts and green leafy vegetables.

CALCIUM

Calcium is the main structural material in bones and teeth and is the most abundant mineral in the body. It helps to control muscle contractions and regulates many of the body's chemical reactions.

Women have greater calcium requirements than men. However, calcium requirements are minimal except when you are growing, pregnant or nursing.

Calcium is not decreased by increased exercise. Almost no calcium is lost in sweat or urine. The only place calcium is lost is through your stool.

There is no such thing as a single pill that contains all the minerals that the body needs in all the right proportions. Manufacturers of such attempts haven't even done particularly well in supplying some of the major minerals. Potassium pills can cause intestinal ulcer, in liquid form it has a foul taste.

Unless it is bound to protein, magnesium cannot be given in pill form because it is poorly absorbed by the body and can cause diarrhea.

The only way to guarantee that you are getting all the minerals you need, including the trace elements, is to eat a well-balanced diet rich in fruit and vegetables, nuts and grains, dairy, and poultry products.

Chapter Seven

Advanced Walking

For those of you who find that you enjoy walking but would also like to satisfy some measure of competitive feelings surging within you, those feelings that drive you to continue to improve and build upon your walking successes, this chapter is for you.

In this chapter, I will give you some idea of how to increase your routine until you are performing at an advanced level—working on fast walking, power walking and racewalking.

For those of you whose primary interest is walking for pleasure and for the health benefits your walking routine brings you, read the chapter anyway. You may find a technique, a variation that will allow you to keep your own walking routine fresh and enjoyable.

FAST WALKING

Yes, fast walking is essentially exactly what it sounds like it would be, walking fast. But not that breathless, sweaty walking that too many of us have experienced on city streets as we've rushed to make an appointment or catch a bus that is about to pull away from the curb. No, this fast walking is a way to push yourself in your walking routine, gradually increasing both your speed and your stamina as you do so.

Fast walking is defined as walking between 3.5 and 4.96 miles per hour. To give you an idea of what this speed means, it is a fast pace that can be done in business clothes. Speeds of over five miles per hour constitute race walking, which I'll get into later.

In order to talk about fast walking, I have to return to a term that hasn't been used since the early chapters of the book, that being aerobics. Unfortunately, many people have come to associate speed with aerobic exercise. They believe that if the activity is 'fast enough' it is aerobic and conversely, if the activity is not 'fast enough' they don't enjoy any aerobic benefits.

Of course, we know that this is incorrect. Aerobic activity only requires that your heart rate increase to its target zone during the activity. This can be achieved by either speed, additional burden (weighting) or walking up a steep incline.

When you begin to perform aerobic walking you are no longer simply maintaining good health, you are burning more calories, building greater muscle tone and increasing your endurance.

Fast walking is an aerobic activity that confers upon you these benefits. (Obviously, if you combine fast walking with weight walking you will increase the benefits.)

One of the most important things you can do to increase your walking speed is to increase the pumping speed of your arms. As your arms go, so go your legs. Bent arms will enable you to walk faster but if you are 'fast walking' on your way to work it might get you some strange stares so you might be more comfortable with straight arms.

When monitoring your increasing speed you can use either the steps-per-minute method or a pedometer.

The basic way to begin to fast walk is to...*walk faster*. But of course, that doesn't tell the whole story.

One way to increase your walking speed is to 'walk sprint'—speeding up for short bursts of distance.

Sprints are quick bursts of speed (as fast as you can go) for very limited distances. While in the process of increasing your walk speed, sprint walking can be repeated 5 to 10 times an hour of walking time. These sprints should last between 30 and 60 seconds for each 6 — 12 minutes of regular walking.

Start your sprint walking by trying to walk 100 yards at 120 steps a minute (or two steps a second). Do this 8 — 20 times depending on your current stamina and health. Try it two to three times a week at first. When you're somewhat comfortable with that, increase the distance in 100 yard lengths every week to two weeks. Do this until you are able to sprint walk 880 yards or one half mile without stopping. Try to increase your steps per minute in increments of two to six steps every two weeks.

Whenever your training becomes too difficult at the increased speed, decrease your DISTANCE and work your way back up again.

Another method of increasing your aerobic walking activity is to 'power walk'—walk with weights attached to your arms and ankles. Those of you who have ever back-packed, carried your own golf bag or portaged a canoe over land, know that weight-loaded walking is much more difficult and requires much more energy than walking unencumbered.

Wrist and ankle weights create the same effect. They increase the work required to walk and therefore the cardiovascular endurance while also providing overall muscle strength.

Of course, as you move up the ladder of speed walking and power walking you will arrive at the top rung—racewalking.

Racewalking is to exercise walking what running is to jogging. The primary differences between racewalking and regular walking is that in racewalking the front foot must touch the ground before the rear foot is lifted and the leg must be fully locked at the knee in the support phase of the stride.

Racewalkers tend to pay more attention to their arm swing than other fast walkers, but their hands do not reach higher or farther back than the chest. Finally, the racewalker tries to make his stride as long as possible by rotating his hip forward and down.

Watching a racewalker, you have the impression that the hip is swinging from side to side. In fact, it moves down and forward.

By applying and practicing these special techniques, a racewaker can walk approximately twice as fast as the average fast walker.

The racewalker begins each stride with a straight leg to achieve maximum pulling power and to avoid creeping—walking with bent knees, not unlike Groucho Marx's famous film walk.

Racewalking, like any form of advanced competitive sport, is best learned by studying with a qualified coach.

Finally, you might want to learn how you can meet other walkers. Maybe you've exhausted all your friends in your neighborhood. Maybe you're looking for more distant pastures to stride. Maybe you just want to meet people who share a common interest in walking and a desire to get the most out of their lives. The best way to do this is to contact any of a number of walking clubs that might be operating in your area.

One way to locate them, of course, is to look in the phone book. But what I think is a nicer way, one that has a number of benefits, is to meet other walkers by participating in any number of 'walking tours' that are held in almost every community in the country. These tours are especially interesting if you live in the city because while on them, you get to explore aspects of the city that you probably never knew existed.

Indeed, it might seem like the most obvious thing to do while on vacation—walk and explore the town. But many of us never get around to doing that at home.

Two sources of walking tour information are a local Chamber of Commerce and also, a local office of the YMCA, YWCA, YHMA, or YHWA.

By the way, if your goal is a walking tour without meeting people; *The Complete Book of Walking* by Charles T. Kintzleman and the editors of *Consumer Guide,* provides a nice listing of various walking tours.

Chapter Eight

Get Out and Walk!

Like the chapter title, what this book is really all about is trying to convince you to get up from your bed, chair, hammock, lethargy, blues, troubles, stresses and to find a beautiful thing that is also good for you.

Basically, I believe that life is too short to waste it needlessly, too short to be wasted being overweight, being unhealthy, being depressed.

What I want to say is that there are beautiful things all around you—enjoy them! Smell those flowers! And do yourself a favor at the same time.

I've outlined many of the things that make walking the perfect activity/exercise in our minds. The basic one, above and beyond all the good it does you, is that it is an activity that you can live with. Say that out loud, *you can live with*.

We recall when we were young having our parents try to convince us to take up a hobby that can be enjoyed even when we grew older (dirt bike racing was out for obvious reasons). We never did find that hobby (they were thinking of something along the lines of stamp collecting) but we have found something that I believe is just as long-lasting and even more beneficial.

Walking increases your sense of well-being. I have friend, call him Bill. Bill is a very successful business man. He is well-liked and well-respected in the community. He coached his sons' Little League teams, he showed up whenever he was able to PTA meetings, he went to open houses at the school. He never forgot his anniversary and his wife was and remains a very lovely, devoted lady.

But Bill felt it all slipping away. When he confided this feeling to me I wasn't sure how to react. After all, Bill was almost the epitome of the model citizen. He was telling me that he felt he was losing a grasp on all those good things.

"Oh, don't get me wrong," he cautioned. "I know how good I have it. It's just...I don't know. I feel like I don't have the same control over my life as I once did.

"To make matters worse, I don't even think I can do anything about it. I mean, everyone has such high expectations of me I feel like I'd be letting them down if I even admitted anything was less than perfect."

I didn't know what to say to Bill so what I did was invite him to accompany me on my walk the following morning.

He looked suspicious. "Walk? That's all you do?"

I nodded. He seemed to be considering all the aspects.

"I really should mow the lawn...."

"Bill," I said, cutting him off. "Do this for you. Just for you. Okay. It'll only be an hour or so. What d'you say?"

He said, "Yes." I picked him up the following morning and drove out to a golf course just out of town.

"I played here once with a client," he said, shaking his head. "I had a terrible back nine. I know I'm supposed to let the client win but I really did do badly."

"Well, never mind that," I said cheerfully. "There are no losers in walking."

I had spent a good deal of time the night before mulling over what Bill had said to me and the more I thought, the more I was convinced that Bill would benefit from a walking program.

We walked that morning without talking much, just strolling at an even, easy pace. It was a beautiful morning, by nine o'clock it was almost seventy degrees. The sky was a clear blue and the first roses were beginning to bloom.

I had my first inkling that the walk was a positive experience for Bill when he mentioned, "You do this regularly?"

"You make it sound like I'm cutting school or something. Yes, I do this every day. At least, I try to."

He shook his head and smiled. A short distance later, he pointed out a butterfly bouncing from tree to tree. "You know, it seems like I haven't seen a butterfly since I was a kid."

Towards the end of the walk, Bill was pointing out flowers and plants that he remembered the names of from when his grandfather had taught him years before. He commented on how beautiful the hills looked against the clear sky.

As we ended our circuit and returned to the car, Bill thanked me.

"I feel...I don't know how to describe it... young again. Younger. I don't know...hopeful somehow." Then he looked at me. "Could I walk with you again?"

"Sure." I smiled.

That was three years ago. Since that time I walk fairly regularly with Bill but quite honestly, he's grown even more dedicated than I. Oh, he still tries to maintain his busy schedule and keeps everyone happy and amazed at how happy he is but he reserves his walks as time for himself and his own thoughts. "My moving meditation," he calls them.

What Bill experienced and experiences today is something that many walkers report—that since walking regularly they have a whole new sense of themselves and the world around them. The psychologists would say that they have an increased sense of well-being but Bill would just sluff that off.

Walking helps reduce the risk of heart attack. Studies have shown that those who lead a sedentary life style are at greater risk of heart disease than those who are active. Unfortunately, many people involve themselves in activities that are too difficult and too stressful for them—thereby increasing rather than decreasing the risk of heart disease. Walkers rarely find themselves in that situation. Walking is an enjoyable, self-paced activity that, in conjunction with a sensible nutritional plan, can greatly reduce the risk of heart attack.

This alone can help you have a better sense of well-being, just knowing that you are doing something positive to prevent a debilitating or fatal disease.

As some of us begin to reach those 'middle' years and above, our thoughts do turn to some of the health related disasters that could confront us. And unfortunately, for many of them we are limited in our methods of prevention. But for heart disease there are things to do that are preventive. Exercise is one and nutrition is another.

And if you have suffered a heart attack, walking is one of the activities that can help you to rehabilitate.

But walking's greatest beauty might not lie in those objective measures at all. It might be impossible to quantify what walking could really do for you.

What our friend Bill referred to as his 'moving meditation' really does come close to the mark. It's not so much that walking lets you 'get away' from your emotional or physical problems. What it seems to do is to change the environment and give these problems a different, broader context. That alone makes them more manageable.

And of course, walking allows you to appreciate and enjoy your surroundings to a degree you might have forgotten was possible.

When we were young, we couldn't wait to get a bicycle and then a car and then a faster car, never noting that the faster the vehicle, the greater the blur the outside world became. Sometimes it is a good thing to slow it down.

A walking tour of our city enables us to see and appreciate architecture and neighborhoods that we might never even have noticed from our cars.

Walking lets us see the world around us and see that it is, or certainly can be, a beautiful world. There are wonders surrounding you but you have to be prepared to look and take note.

Maybe the bottom truth is that walking, for all its other benefits, allows us the freedom to take note. To take note of the world around us, of ourselves in that world, of what each moment of our lives could and should be.

Walking is a way of taking note. It lets us slow down time, our own and the world's. Walking gives us time to stop and smell the roses.

"I'm just enjoying myself," he'd say, laughing. "Just feeling good."

Another friend, Judy, used to complain about a nearly insatiable desire for junk food. "I'm going to a hypnotist," she said. "I saw an advertisement in the paper. Money back guarantee. I'm really going to go."

I convinced her to try walking with me before she went to the hypnotist. Since walking, her desire for junk food has decreased.

"I still love it when I can get it," she says, smiling sheepishly. "But I don't seem to *need* it, you know?"

I nodded my head.

Walking does accomplish these things, it does increase your sense of well-being, it does decrease your desire to eat junk foods. No, this is not another 'we can solve the problems of the world' claim. There is no magic. The explanation is fairly straightforward.

The issue is control. Control of your life and your appetites. Any time you can impose an order to your life, whether it is by reading a book every day or by walking seven miles, you will increase your sense of control. This helps control your mental outlook and those cravings that are a result of the sense of helplessness that grows from feeling you have no control.

The problem is that many of the things people do and try to get control of eventually defeat them—that is, they either require cowing to some authority or require too much of a money investment in fancy clothes or something. Either that or the activity itself is too demanding or becomes boring.

Walking avoids the entire problem. It is an activity that you control. For the most part it is highly individual, the routine and program are all yours. And, as an activity, as I've said before, it can stay with you all your life.

In addition, walking has all the benefits of exercise. It's no wonder that I blow my bugle for walking, is it?

Walking does help to create a better, more positive self image. How? Well for starters, it makes you feel better because you look better. Who wouldn't feel better if they could get up in the morning and look at themselves in the mirror and say, "You look good." Who among us wouldn't feel good if we could put on a pair of pants or a skirt and realize that the waist is an inch or two too large? Who among us wouldn't feel good if someone in our office commented about how healthy we were looking or if we had changed our hairstyle or whatever people say when they're trying to put their finger on whatever it is that shows about how you feel better?

Walking helps us lose those inches, that slouch, that extra chin, those worry lines on our foreheads, that cloud of stressfulness. Walking helps us to look better and, at least in the world we inhabit, looking better helps us to feel better.

Walking helps us to become physically fit.

We all enjoy feeling fit. Who wouldn't want to be able to

climb the stairs without getting winded or play with their grandchildren without feeling physically wiped out? All of this is a function of how fit we are, how our endurance is. Walking improves endurance. It increases circulation, increases bone mass, strengthens bones and tendons, loosens joints—helps us to become physically fit.

Special Reference Section

Although I've gone to great lengths to describe the benefits and the joys of walking, especially as it compares to running or any other exercise program, walking is still exercise, it still utilizes your body system and it still relies on your muscular and skeletal system. Therefore, there is still the possibility of injury.

Most walker injuries are minor, falling somewhere in the 'blister—corn' category. However, if your posture or walking technique is very far off 'normal' you could be putting undue stress on your bones and muscles, causing more serious injury. If this is the case, or if you ever have any injury that seems to persist or causes you too much discomfort—see your doctor. If you don't have a doctor to check with for such injuries, call a podiatrist. He or she is uniquely qualified to attend to such injuries.

I list below some of the injuries or conditions that you might confront as a walker along with a description of exactly what the condition is.

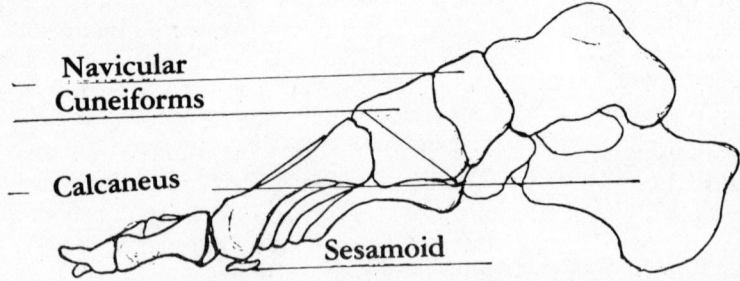

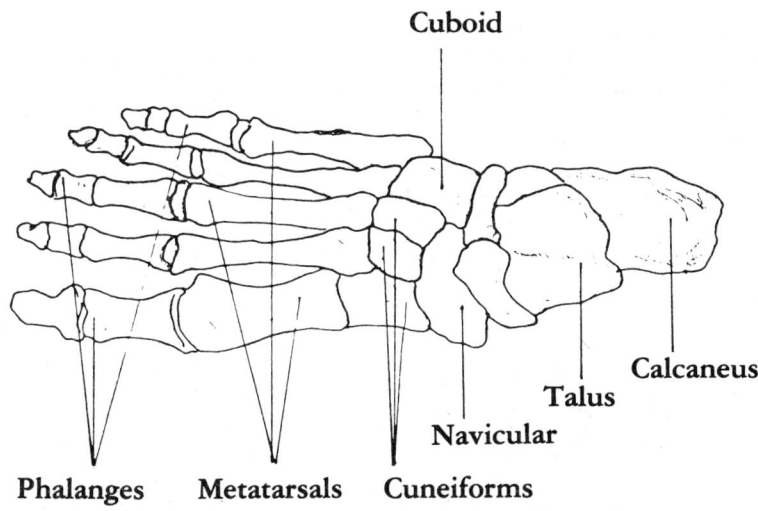

The first and probably most common of all 'injuries' and one that you have already experienced during your lifetime is blisters.

Blisters

Blisters plague everyone sometime. They are irritating and annoying and can make walking a painful rather than enjoyable experience. Blisters are caused by pressure and friction on pressure points or on bony prominences. As the skin rubs against skin the outer layer of skin becomes pulled away from the deeper layers. The separated skin bubbles up and fills with a clear fluid which is actually cellular fluid from injured cells.

Blisters tend to occur on skin areas that are not accustomed to pressure. That is why they tend to appear when you get a new pair of shoes that don't fit your foot just right or when you begin a new activity such as walking. Each activity has different 'stress points' where blisters frequently appear. For example, a raquetball player usually gets blisters on the insides of his great toes. As the skin toughens, blisters occur less frequently.

People who suffer from chronic blisters should wear two pairs of socks—dress socks next to the skin and athletic socks on top. That way, the friction occurs between the two layers of socks rather than the layers of skin.

Some people simply apply gobs of petrolatum (vaseline or its generic) to their feet to eliminate friction.

If you should get a blister, treat it as soon as possible. Allowing a blister to remain and get irritated could invite infection. If you treat the blister early, it is a simple matter easily remedied.

Do not remove the skin over the blister! Beneath this top layer the skin is sensitive and raw and irritated. Instead, drain the blister with a sterile needle (heated until it's red by fire and then wiped with rubbing alcohol). To drain a blister simply puncture the top layer of the bubble. This will cause absolutely no pain as the skin is dead. To better insure drainage puncture two holes in the bubble. Be careful not to prick the sensitive tissue underneath.

After draining apply an antibiotic ointment or cream. On top of this place cotton over just the area of the blister. Then apply tape or moleskin to hold the cotton in place. The cotton keeps the loose top of the blister from sticking to the tape or moleskin.

Do not remove the top of the blister! It will come off when the blister heals. The healing should take about two weeks but you will be ready to continue normal activity as soon as you complete the above treatment.

Corns

Another irritation that is caused primarily from friction is a corn. Corns are painful skin lesions that have been around from the time human beings first put shoes on their feet. The corn is caused primarily by friction and pressure between a toe and the shoe. Pressure from the shoe initiates a response in the skin to protect itself.

The skin protects itself by producing more cells from the basal layer of the skin. As the skin thickens itself in response to pressure it forms the corn.

Relief is brought about by the removal of the pressure—such as throwing away the shoes that fit too tightly. Padding the area may be of some help but avoid the medicated pads that tout themselves as corn removers. The medications on the pads contain

SOFT CORN

acid which eats through the layers of flesh of the corn. Although this is effective, unfortunately, acid is not an intelligent substance. It doesn't know how to tell the difference between healthy tissue and the corn. Therefore, it continues to eat away at your toe after it has done whatever benefit it can. This can create an infection that has to be treated with antibiotics.

A pumice stone is sometimes effective in removing some of the excess tissue but the best thing to do if you have a bothersome corn is to consult a foot specialist who is expert at treating these painful conditions.

Another kind of corn is referred to as a 'soft corn'. Soft corns usually occur between the 4th and 5th toes or between the 3rd and 4th toes. These corns are sometimes referred to as 'kissing corns' because they result from the pressing together of the two affected toes.

These soft corns have a whitish appearance which leads some to believe that they are infections with fungus or yeast. Mistreated, they do sometimes evolve into such infections but basically, they are not.

These corns should be treated and removed by a podiatrist. In addition, an x-ray may reveal a bony protrusion or exostosis which is responsible for the condition. If this proves to be the case, the protrusion can be safely removed in a podiatrist's office using local anesthesia.

Dermatitis

In addition to these painful skin irritations there is a class of general skin irritation referred to as dermatitis. There are as many forms of dermatitis that affect the foot as affect the rest of the body. There are contact dermatitis' from the tanning chemicals from the leather in shoes, from laundry detergents, from the synthetic materials that modern day shoes are made from.

Psoriasis affects the feet and nails. Athlete's foot which is caused by a fungus is a common skin problem. It also affects the toenails, as does yeast.

There are an enormous number of skin conditions that affect the foot. Unfortunately, walking, or any activity which causes your feet to sweat will make the condition more irritated. If you do have a skin condition on your feet, consult your podiatrist. He or she will be able to treat it and have you back out on the trails in no time!

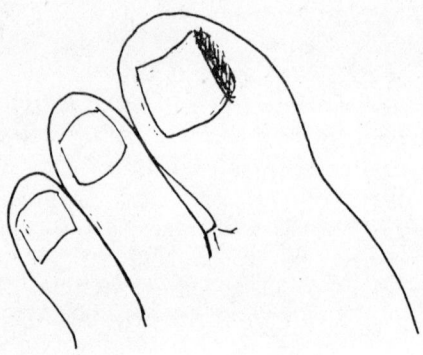

Ingrown Toenails

Another injury or condition that can make your walking jaunt agony is ingrown toenails. Ingrown toenails occur when the side of the nail digs into the adjacent flesh, causing discomfort. If the condition progresses the edge of the nail may penetrate the flesh. This can result in pain and subsequent infection.

This condition is hereditary, the result primarily of toenail curvature. Improperly fitting shoes that exert pressure to the side of the toe make the condition worse. Oftentimes, ingrown toenails are triggered by getting your toes stepped on.

There are various forms of treatment. Removal of the nail is not the best, since when the nail regrows it will simply grow in again to the same condition. One treatment with a high degree of success is to excise the affected nail border while using a local anesthetic and then to treat the offending nail root by using a laser which vaporizes the cells that are growing the offending portion of the nail.

Obviously, if you are suffering from ingrown toenails it is best to seek out your foot specialist as soon as possible.

Fungus Toenails

Another condition that can cause pain is fungus toenails. Fungus toenails appear as yellow or white streaks in the nail plate. A nail affected with fungus may have a white or yellow chalky appearance on its surface. Do not neglect this condition because it becomes progressively harder to treat.

Unfortunately, many people are erroneously told that there is nothing that can be done about this condition. This is not true. The difficulty in treating fungus toenails is in identifying the fungus itself. To do this a culture must be taken and then an appropriate medication can be prescribed.

The treatment of choice doesn't usually involve removal of the toenail. Rather, the use of a laser combined with the use of topical medications is the treatment of choice. The treatment time is from seven months to a year or more to completely eliminate the condition. In the most stubborn cases, oral medications are used.

Callouses

Callouses are another annoying problem that many people suffer. Like many of the other ailments that can cause you problems while walking, callouses are also caused by friction and pressure. Responding to the pressure from shoes, the skin thickens itself as a form of protection against the increased stress. Callouses occur on the ball of the foot, on the heels, on the inside of the foot where bunions occur, on the outside of the foot where a bunionette might occur, and occasionally on the bottom of the foot as with the case of an acquaintance of ours. She had the callous as the result of a bone spur growing down from the bottom of the 3rd metatarsal.

Callouses also occur on the medial or inside border of the great toe especially in people with flat feet or that pronate excessively in gait.

Callouses can be especially painful when they get excessively thickened and then get a blister beneath them. Don't neglect callouses so that they progress to a painful condition. Treatment can be by smoothing the excess tissue with a pumice stone. Check your shoes for proper fit.

A particularly painful callous should be checked by a podiatrist to differentiate it from a wart which is of viral origin.

If the callous is caused by a prominent metatarsal, a biomechanical orthotic device may be employed to transfer pressure away from the offending metatarsal. If a metatarsal is greatly deviated from a normal position, a surgical procedure could be employed to remove the excessive stress from the metatarsal bones. The condition of excess callouses should be treated by a podiatrist who possesses the skill and equipment necessary to successfully deal with the problem.

Warts

Warts, or verruca, are soft, spongy, well-defined growths caused by the human papilloma virus. They are well supplied with blood vessels as can be seen by the little black, brown or red dots at the center of the lesion. Warts can be very disabling depending on the site. They can be found anywhere on the foot. On top of the foot the growths protrude and have the familiar cauliflower appearance, but standing causes warts to grow into the foot. These lesions are called 'plantar warts' and the term 'plantar' refers to the bottom of the foot and has no agricultural signficance whatsoever.

Warts are often mistaken for corns and callouses, but they can be distinguished from each other in several ways. Corns and callouses are always found on pressure points whereas warts may be seen on all parts of the foot. The fingerprint-like ridges are displaced by warts but remain intact with callouses. By far the best way to determine if you have a wart is to pinch it from side to side. A sharp pain will result from an active wart while corns and callouses will be more sensitive to direct pressure.

If a wart is persistent or it it starts to spread, it should be treated as soon as possible. Self-treatment is not recommended since 'bathroom surgery' can lead to extensive bleeding and infection.

The podiatrist has several ways to deal with with warts, most of which involve removing the virus infected tissue. A wart can be frozen, treated with acid, but by far the quickest way to take care of a wart is by laser excision in the doctor's office.

After numbing the area with a local anesthetic, the doctor dissects the wart from the normal tissue with a special laser instrument and then he or she applies an acid to kill any viral particles that may remain. The success rate is very high with this quick and painless procedure.

Ganglionic Cysts

Ganglionic cysts by their very nature create a stress and pressure point. These cysts form on or around a tendon or joint capsule. The cyst is actually a ballooning of the tendon sheath or capsular tissues and is filled with a gelatinous fluid.

The cysts may also increase in size with activity. This is because more fluid is produced inside the cyst during activity.

The most common areas of occurrence are the wrist, ankle and the foot.

Treatment of these cysts is by draining the fluid or by breaking the walls of the cysts by pressure. One of the old methods that is not advocated by us was to hit the cyst with a book so as to burst it under the skin. Thus ruptured, the cyst would be gone. I do not advocate this 'interesting' and somewhat medieval treatment for the simple reason that it is too easy to cause more extensive damage by employing it.

The cyst may be surgically excised. This is a delicate procedure because the surgeon must identify and tie off the stalk from which the cyst grows. There is, unfortunately, a high incidence or reccurrence with this type of growth.

Bunions

Bunions are large prominences of bone on the outside of the great toe joint. They are caused by the progressive movement of the great toe towards the second toe with the formation of an over growth of bone either of the side or the top of the great toe joint. Bunions may be hereditary. It is not uncommon to see entire families with similar bunion deformities.

A bunion is a progressive problem and like most problems, does not go away by itself.

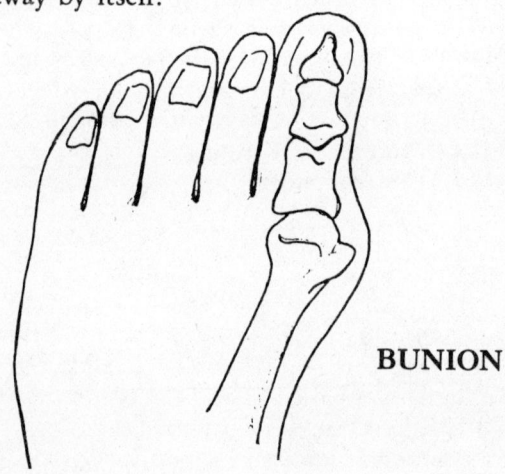

BUNION

One way to minimize the discomfort brought on by a bunion is to wear wider shoes. This helps to relieve some of the pressure from the area. In addition, it is possible that placing a pad around the bunion will help. If the area is extremely inflamed, an injection with an anti-inflammatory medication may provide relief.

If none of these symptomatic treatments works then the patient has the option of surgical removal of the bunion.

There are many types of bunion surgery and each has to be tailored to the specific problems of the individual. There does not exist a single surgical procedure applicable to all bunions.

One type of procedure does not require a cast but only a bandage for an approximate two-week period. Other procedures require 5 — 6 weeks of casting. Some procedures can be performed in the doctor's office under local anesthetic while more complicated ones are best done in a hospital setting.

Each bunion deformity must be evaluated on an individual basis using x-ray examination, the individual patient's history and a medical evaluation.

Tailor's Bunion

A different type of bunion, commonly referred to as a bunionette or a tailor's bunion, is located on the opposite side of the foot from the bunion. The term, 'tailor's bunion' came from the days of the tailor who sewed everything by hand. As he would sit cross-legged on the floor, the outside of his foot would rub on the floor and cause pressure and subsequently a sore enlargement would form which was painful.

The tailor's bunion or bunionette is much like a bunion in its cause and formation. However, they are on a much smaller scale.

Treatment for a bunionette is very similar to that of a bunion, beginning with wider shoes, padding, injections and finally a surgical procedure.

Surgical removal is much easier on a bunionette than on a bunion because it is a smaller deformity. Also, often a soft tissue growth is associated with the tailor's bunion which is responsible for its increased size.

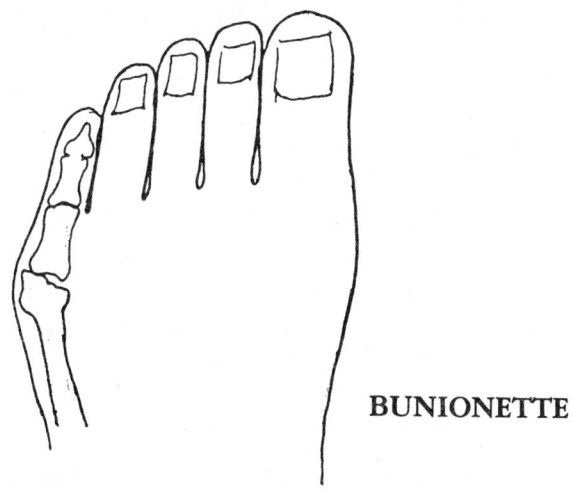

BUNIONETTE

Hammertoes

Hammertoe is a deformity of the toe where a buckling of the toe has occurred and the middle joint of the toe sticks up and rubs on the shoe. Hammertoes are sometimes hereditary but most often are associated with poor foot structure and function. Shoes are often contributory. A tight fitting shoe pushes the toes into this deformed state.

Besides being painful where the bone rubs the shoe, it is painful to be walking on the end of the toe and sometimes the toenail.

Treatment is by wearing shoes wide enough and with a deep enough toebox to accommodate the deformity. Pads sometimes help. Sometimes a crest pad is used to hold the toe straight.

If the hammertoe is flexible or reducible, which means it can be easily straightened with your fingers, then a simple procedure can be performed to lengthen the tendons on the top and on the bottom of the toe. These tendons may be contracted and are the deforming force causing the poor position of the toe.

Other hammertoes that are not flexible might have to be straightened by working on the toe joint. A hammertoe correction is a simple procedure and can be performed in the office setting using only local anesthesia.

As you can see, many foot ailments are the result of a poor choice of shoe—either by style or fit. It is just as important that you take the same care choosing your working or everyday shoes as you do in choosing your walking shoe!

Shin Splints

Another ailment that occasionally plagues walkers and runners is shin splints. 'Shin Splints' is a catch-all phrase which is greatly misunderstood because the two most common shin splint variations are anterior and posterior tibial shin splints. Anterior shin splints occur on the front outside part of the leg and involve the anterior tibial muscle and tendon. The function of the anterior tibial muscle and tendon is to decelerate the foot at heel strike and to prevent the foot from 'slapping' down to the ground. Anterior tibial shin splints occur when the anterior tibial muscle is weak and the opposing muscles, the gastrocnemius and soleus, are too tight. The most common cure for this type of shin splint is to stretch the posterior group and to strengthen the anterior tibial muscle by dorsiflexion weight training. Heel lifts, a change in shoe gear or orthotics may be necessary.

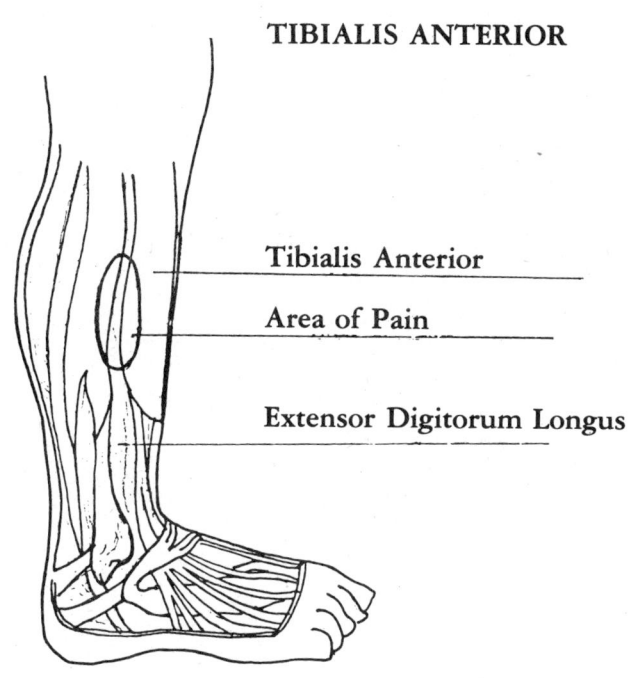

TIBIALIS ANTERIOR

Posterior tibial shin splints occur at the lower inside part of the leg. The function of the involved muscle is to hold the arch of the foot up during the weightbearing phase of gait. This muscle prevents the foot from over-pronating or flattening. Thus, the cure for this type of shin splint is to prevent pronation using different shoes or biomechanical orthotics to control the function

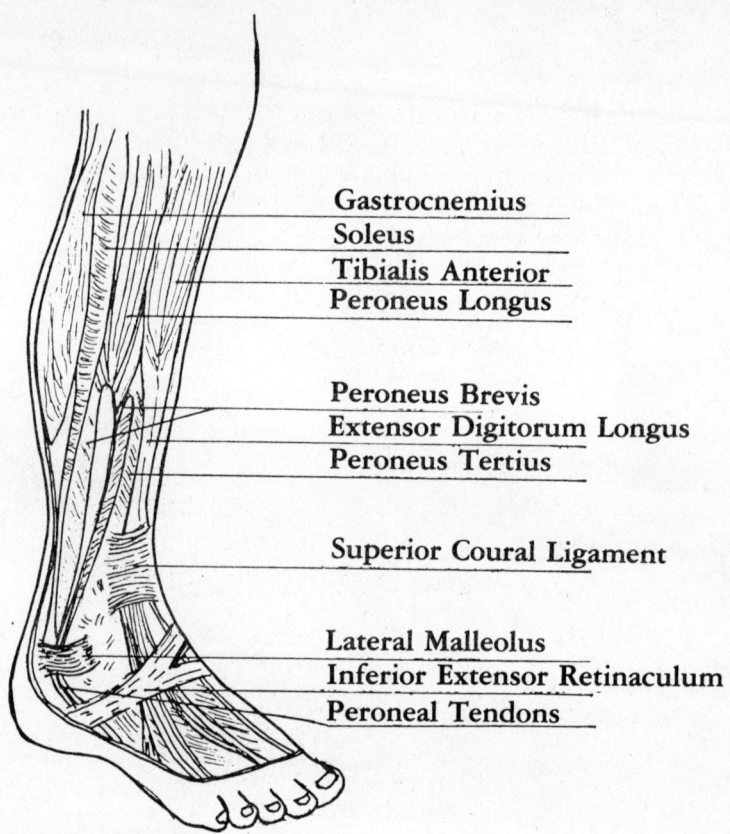

of the foot. Stretching of the posterior muscle group may also be helpful.

Achilles Tendonitis

Achilles tendonitis is a condition in which the Achilles tendon becomes irritated at or near its insertion into the heel bone. People suffering from this condition may have tight calf muscles, or their foot may pronate excessively during the midstance phase of gait. Women who are accustomed to wearing high heeled shoes and then change to low heeled shoes may experience this discomfort because their calf muscles have become contracted by the constant wearing of high heels.

Treatment is by stretching, utilizing contrast baths, physical therapy such as ultrasound, changing foot gear, or the use of biomechanical orthotics to control the pronation of the foot. When a foot is over pronating, the heel bone is moving excessively and this movement may set up a mechanical irritation at the insertion of the Achilles tendon into the calcaneus.

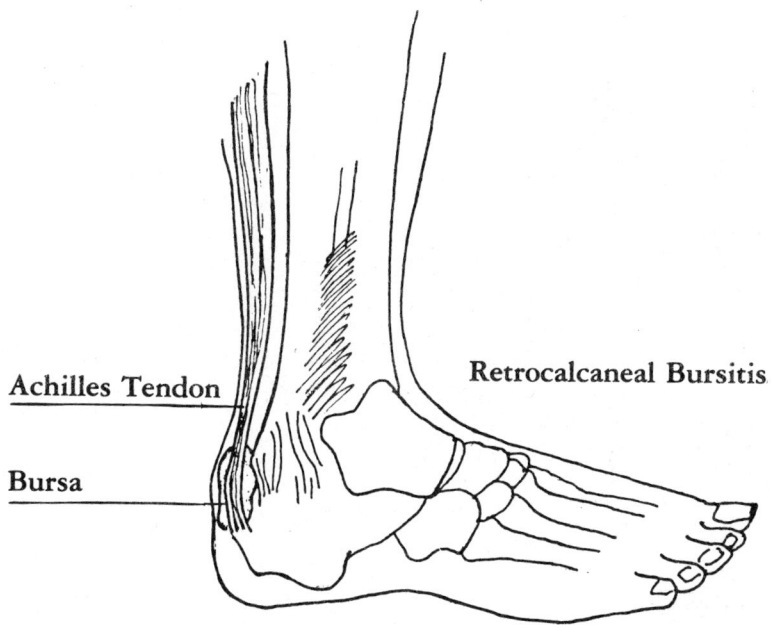

Walker's Knee

Those who walk extended mileage and whose feet pronate excessively may suffer this condition where the cartilage on the underside of the kneecap becomes excessively and unevenly worn. It may be caused by the foot pronating excessively, allowing the leg and knee to internally rotate an excessive amount. With the knee functioning in this position, the contraction of the quadriceps of the thigh muscle create a sideways pull on the kneecap, or patella, which results in excessive forces on the underside and lateral aspect of the kneecap, resulting in irritation. This condition is also known as chondromalacia.

Treatment is by preventing the abnormal function by changing shoes or by using biomechanical orthotics to control the weightbearing position of the foot and leg. Sometimes, antiinflammatory oral medications may be necessary to reduce the inflammation.

Retro Calcaneal Bursitis

A bursa is a fluid-filled sac which cushions a tendon where it moves over a bone. When overuse occurs, this protective sac becomes inflamed, painful and increases in size. Such a bursal sac can occur where the Achilles tendon rubs over the posterior aspect of the calcaneus. Treatment is by physical therapy and by reducing the movement of the tendon over the heel bone by using biochemechanical orthotics.

Sometimes, oral or injectable anti-inflammatory medications are necessary to control the pain. In extreme conditions, surgical excision of the bursa with remodeling of the bone may be necessary.

Painful Os Navicularis

As I discussed above in regards to posterior tibial tendon shin splints, the posterior tibial tendon functions to hold the arch of the foot up during the weightbearing phase of the gait. When the foot pronates excessively, the posterior tibial muscle and tendon unit pulls on the navicular bone to stop the foot from flattening.

If the situation of over-pronation is allowed to continue, irritation may occur at the insertion of the tendon into the bones. The pain of this condition is located at the inside of the arch of the foot and the navicular bone is usually tender to direct pressure. The simplest treatment is by preventing the over-pronation using biomechanical orthotics and physical therapy.

Poor quality shoes can also contribute to this condition. In some cases, an extra bone is present at the tendon insertion. This extra bone is called the os tibialis externium and in some resistant cases, has to be removed.

Ankle sprains

One of the most common injuries to the ankle is the inversion sprain where the foot and ankle are tipped inward.

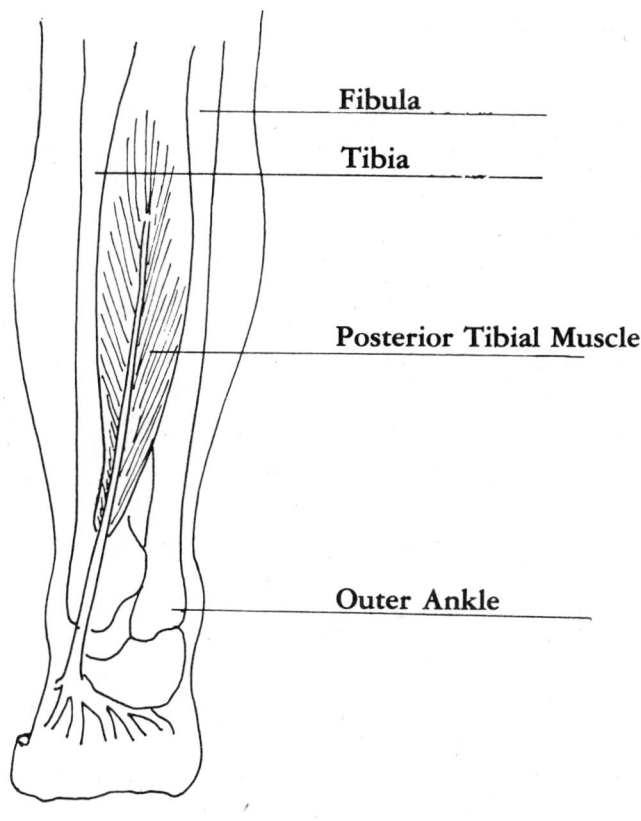

Immediately, the pain is present on the outside of the ankle bone. An ankle sprain is best treated professionally by a doctor totally familiar with this injury. Most likely, x-rays will be necessary to rule out a fracture of the ankle bones and some of the bones in the foot. The doctor can then advise you if the injury is mild, moderate, or severe and instruct you as to how to care for it to prevent permanent damage to the area.

Plantar Fasciitis

One of the most common foot injuries is plantar fasciitis, which is a strain of the ligamentous structure which serves to support the longitudinal arch of the foot. The plantar fascia is a tough, fibrous band of connective tissue which extends from the base of the toes to the calcaneus on the bottom of the foot.

As stress is applied to the foot there is a tendency for the foot to collapse and attempt to elongate in response to the increased stress of body weight which is applied during the weight bearing phase of gait. As this stress is applied to the inelastic ligament during weight bearing, microtrauma or tearing of the fibers of the ligaments may result.

Symptomatically, this is experienced by the patient as a pain in the longitudinal arch of the foot. The pain is often described as a sharp and sometimes burning feeling which causes them to limp in an attempt to relieve the pressure on the ligament. The pain causes some to walk on the outside of the foot in an attempt to transfer this stress to another area of the foot.

Treatment for this condition is in the form of increasing the support to the longitudinal arch of the foot to take the stress away from the plantar fascia. This can be accomplished by changing the shoe to a shoe with greater support in the longitudinal arch, placing felt pads beneath the longitudinal arch, taping the foot to prevent the stress and on a more permanent basis, the use of a biomechanical orthotic which is made from a plaster impression of the foot.

Calcaneal Spur (Heel Spur) Or Calcaneal Periostitis

This condition has the same cause as plantar fasciitis except with continued stress, the plantar fascia pulls with such great force at its insertion into the heel bone (calcaneus) that it will partially pull loose from the bone by pulling the outer covering of the bone (periosteum) away from the bone itself.

This condition or state is termed calcaneal periostitis. What happens next is that the area where the periosteum has pulled away from the bones exhibits bleeding and inflammation occurs. If this injury is allowed to continue over an extended period, the area where the bleeding occurs calcifies and subsequently appears on an x-ray as a heel spur.

Patients with this condition report that the plantar surface or bottom of the heel feels like a stone bruise. The area of maximum tenderness is felt most often directly in the center of the plantar surface of the heel where the bone is.

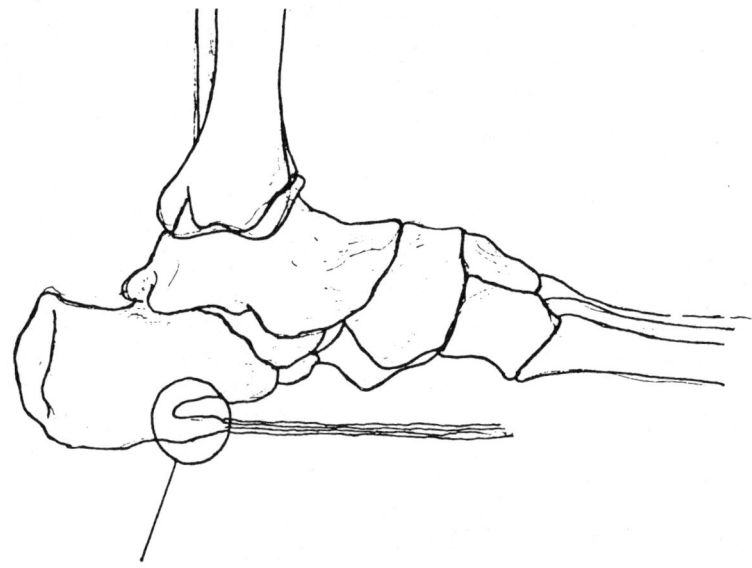

Calcaneal Spur

Sometimes the pain is more to the medial or inside of the heel where the medial slip of the plantar fascia inserts.

Treatment consists of using a shoe with more support for the arch of the foot and sometimes an additional felt pad in this area may help.

Occasionally anti-inflammatory medications are used but often they do not address the biomechanical stress which is the cause of the pain. Biomechanical orthotics will eliminate the pain of the heel spur in approximately 85% of the cases because they will relieve the stress on the plantar fascia which caused the heel spur in the first place.

Sometimes an injection of local anesthetic and a long lasting anti-inflammatory medication is necessary.

Taping helps but it is almost impossible to continually wear tape because it irritates the skin and many patients develop tape dermatitis. Surgical excision is reserved for recalcitrant cases. After surgical excision of the heel spur, the heel will remain tender for two or three months, so this can not be considered an immediate cure.

When the stress can be removed from the area, the pain will subside even though the spur remains visible on an x-ray. The cause of pain is the biomechanical stress and not the heel spur itself.

Sesamoiditis

There are two sesamoid bones under the first metatarsal head which act as part of the pulley mechanism which plantarflexes the great toe. These bones, and more frequently the tibial rather than the fibular one, are subjected to great stress as the great toe plantarflexes during the toe-off phase of gait.

When constant irritation is inflicted on these bones, they may become inflamed which is a state referred to as sesamoiditis.

If the stress is great enough, they could even become fractured. The pain of this condition occurs directly beneath the first metatarsal head and is painful on direct pressure.

Treatment should first be directed to relieving the stress on the bone. A shoe with adequate forefoot padding as well as forefoot flexibility is a must. Felt pads put in such a manner as to relieve the stress are often helpful.

Long term correction of this condition should be in the form of a biomechanical orthotic to transfer the stress away from the area. Sometimes an orthotic with an accommodative depression under this area is necessary. Recalcitrant cases may require oral anti-inflammatory agents and sometimes injection of anti-inflammatory medication is called for. On rare occasions, application of a walking cast is necessary. Surgical excision of the sesamoid has been necessary only on very rare occasions.

Stress Fractures

Stress fractures occur when repeated microtrauma to a bone results in a minute crack in the bone. This is experienced as pain upon weight bearing and pain to the area when touched.

Stress fractures can occur at the calcaneus, each metatarsal, the navicular, the talus, the cuboid, the fibula, the tibia and the femur. I have seen each of these varieties of stress fracture as a result of marching, which creates a particularly brutal stress on the leg and foot.

In addition, many young recruits from the Marine Recruiting Depot in San Diego had been sedentary before induction into the Marines and when forced to march twenty miles, the bone was over stressed and stress fractures occurred.

Symptoms include point tenderness, swelling, inflammation and an inability to continue walking without pain. X-ray examination is usually negative until the bone callous occurs in the second or third week following the injury. Bone scans performed by a radiologist are very helpful in establishing the diagnosis. If the stress fracture is in the leg or thigh, an orthopedist should be called in.

Treatment is by reducing the level of activity, or changing the activity until the fracture heals.

A change of activity to something such as bicycling or swimming will help the bones to heal more quickly. Reducing the stress to the area using padding, taping or biomechanical orthotics will also help. Ice and contrasting warm and cold soaks are also helpful. In very acute instances, anti-inflammatory medicines, either oral or injected, provide rapid relief.

Toe Fractures

This is a very painful injury which should be treated immediately to prevent prolonged agony and later deformity. The old saying that nothing can be done for toe fractures is painfully *untrue*.

The toe should be x-rayed to confirm the fracture. If it is displaced, the toe should be anesthetized with local anesthetic and the fracture reduced. The toe is then splinted with an elastic self-adherent splinting material to maintain the correct alignment.

A displaced digital fracture which is not treated can lead to a permanent deformity. Approximately six weeks are required for a digital fracture to heal.

Neuroma

The third intermetatarsal space is the most common site of occurrence with the second intermetatarsal space a close second. Irritation to the interdigital nerves by friction on the adjacent metatarsal can be triggered by too tight a shoe or by excessive motion of the metatarsal bones of the foot.

What happens is the nerve becomes irritated and subsequently swells and thus causes more pressure on the adjacent bone and tissue. The irritation to the nerve becomes greater and the pain begins.

Many patients describe the pain as a stabbing, sharp pain accompanied at times by numbness and tingling in the toes.

The simplest treatment is to make certain that the shoe is wide enough and is not exerting excessive pressure from the sides on the forefoot which would squeeze the nerve. An injection around the nerve of local anesthetic and an anti-inflammatory medication to eliminate the swelling in the nerve is often called for. Sometimes this injection has to be repeated once a week for three

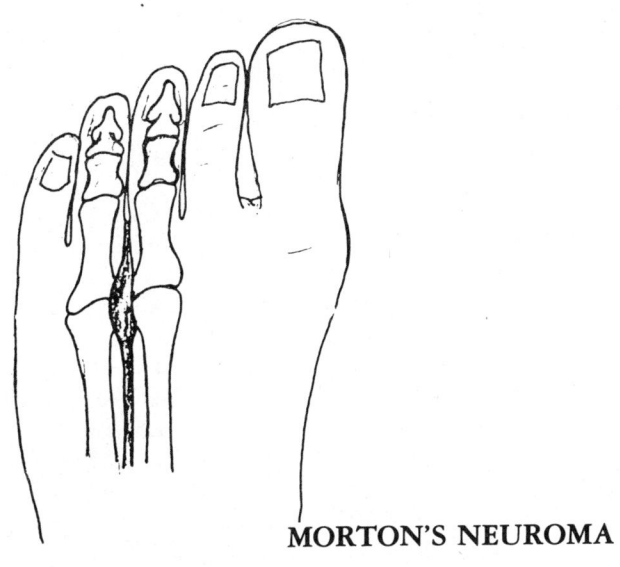

MORTON'S NEUROMA

weeks. An orthotic is very helpful because it reduces the movement of the metatarsal bones which are rubbing on the nerve. Ultrasound physical therapy also helps to reduce the swelling.

If these methods are unsuccessful, sometimes surgical excision is called for. This procedure sometimes leaves the affected toes somewhat numb. However, patients who require such radical treatment usually report that they would rather have the numbness than the sharp pain.

Subungal Exostosis

This is a very painful situation in which the very end of the great toe is very sensitive to pressure from the top. An exostosis or bone spur forms on the distal phalanx underneath the end of the toenail. Pressure of any kind elicits exquisite pain.

Treatment should be in the form of avoiding pressure to the area. Complete relief can be achieved by having the exostosis removed in the office by a doctor using local anesthetic. This is simple procedure which requires only one stitch.

Exostoses of Digits

Exostoses or bone spurs can occur on virtually any bone. They occur with great frequency on the digits in response to shoe pressure. The outer covering of the bone, or periosteum, is sensitive to irritation which is how the body knows when a bone is fractured and is required to send osteoblast cells to the fracture area to heal it.

When the bone is irritated by pressure over a long period of time, the body senses this periosteal irritation and sends osteoblasts to the area. These cells lay down new bone which becomes an exostosis. What results is an irritated area with a bony bump which is then a further source of irritation.

As the skin is irritated by the shoe, the skin responds by thickening itself as a form of self-protection. As the skin continues to thicken, a corn or heloma dura is formed. Arthritis sufferers are especially susceptible to bone spur conditions.

Removal of the irritating exostosis can be accomplished safely in the doctor's office using local anesthetic. The patient will be able to walk out of the office with only a small bandage on the toe.

As can be determined by even a casual reading of the above few pages, almost all of the injuries or conditions described here are the result of stresses and friction that can easily be avoided. *There is no reason to suffer from any of the above ailments.*

Your feet, in fact your entire body, except in rare cases, have been formed to more than adequately serve you in carrying out all forms of reasonable activity.

Don't create a counterproductive situation by forcing your feet into uncomfortable situations. Evaluate your shoes. Are they healthy for your feet? This should be the first question, not, how do they look? As a fashion note, very few people, regardless what they wear, look good when they are grimacing in pain.

Finally, there will be occasions when you will suffer minor injuries while walking that cannot be foreseen. These accidents, such as stepping off a curb, tripping over a child's toy, or twisting an ankle on a small stone in your path, sometimes occur. When they do, there is a simple four-step procedure which you should follow to minimize you own discomfort as well as minimize the chance of further irritation. These four steps can be easily remembered by the acronym: RICE.

R, REST. Rest is necessary because continued activity on the part could cause further injury. Stop activity immediately.

I, ICE. Ice decreases the bleeding from injured blood vessels because it causes them to constrict. The more bleeding that occurs, the longer it takes an injury to heal.

C, COMPRESSION. Compression limits the amount of swelling that can take place. Injured tissues leak fluid and blood into the surrounding areas which cause swelling. The swelling must be controlled in this manner to prevent further injury.

E, ELEVATION. Elevation of the injured part utilizes the forces of gravity to help drain excess fluid from the area.

The RICE program can be utilized for the first twenty-four hours after an injury. Heat should not be applied until after the first forty-eight hours have passed since the heat would make the swelling worse by dilating the blood vessels.

Further treatment depends on the type of tissue that was injured and the severity of the injury. It is wise to have an injured part x-rayed to rule out the possibility of a fracture.

References

Berger, Stuart M. *How To Be Your Own Nutritionist.* (William Morrow and Company)
Block, Dr. Barry H. *Foot Talk.* (Zebra Books)
Cooper, Dr. Kenneth H. *Running Without Fear.* (Bantam Books)
Haas, Dr. Robert. *Eat to Win.* (Signet Books)
Mirkin, Dr. Gabe. *Fitness Clinic.* (Contemporary Press)
Mirkin & Hoffman. *The Sportsmedicine Book.* (Little, Brown)
Morehouse, Laurence E. *Total Fitness in 30 Minutes a Week.* (Pocket Books)
Southmayd, Dr. William. *Sportshealth.* (Perigee Books)
Stutman, Dr. Fred A. *Walk, Don't Die.* (Medical Manor Books)
Subotnick, Steven, D.P.M., M.S. *The Running Foot Doctor.* (World Publications)
Sweetgall, Robert. *Fitness Walking.* (Perigee Books)
Yanker, Gary. *Complete Book of Exercisewalking.* (Contemporary Books)
—. *Walking Workouts.* (Warner Books)